PEAK BRAIN PLASTICITY

REMEMBER WHAT YOU WANT TO REMEMBER AND FORGET WHAT YOU CAN'T FORGET

SAID HASYIM

Edited by
DAVID ARETHA

Hardcover ISBN: 978-981-14-9957-9
Paperback ISBN: 978-981-14-9958-6
E-Book ISBN: 978-981-14-9959-3
Audiobook ISBN: 978-981-14-9960-9

PRAISE FOR PEAK BRAIN PLASTICITY

Unlock the power of your mind with this accessible, thought-provoking tool.

— Wishing Shelf

There is a lot of information to help in making learning easier and also to achieve a peak brain function that will bring out the best in readers.

— Readers' Favorite

The information would be useful to someone who wanted to improve their memory or how their minds work.

— B.R.A.G. Medallion

For you

Take time to sharpen your saw now,

For you will save more time to cut more trees later.

CONTENTS

DISCLAIMER

This book contains advice and information relating to health care. It should be used to supplement rather than replace the advice of your doctor or another trained health professional. If you know or suspect you have a health problem, it is recommended that you seek your physician's advice before embarking on any medical program or treatment. All efforts have been made to assure the accuracy of the information contained in this book as of the date of publication. The author disclaims liability for any medical outcomes that may occur as a result of applying the methods suggested in this book.

INTRODUCTION

Have you come across people who seem to be always sharp, even in their seventies? What about others who have visibly deteriorated brainpower as they age? The former people were not necessarily born with superior genes. They have cultivated lifelong habits that allow them to maintain high-functioning brains, whether or not they are aware of it.

Jack is sixty years old now and frequently forgets what he has been told. He finds it difficult to pick up gardening, even though he'd like to help his wife out with her garden. Learning a foreign language, Japanese, would be the last thing to cross his mind as he thinks his brain wouldn't be able to handle it. Despite that, it would make him thrilled if he could communicate with his five-year-old granddaughter, who was born in Japan and only knows how to speak Japanese.

He reminisces about how he used to be a top student during high school. He always studied hard and scored well on exams. As he entered the workforce, he learned new skills to perform well at work. Occasionally, his company would send him to take courses. After working for over three years, though, there were no new skills for him to learn anymore. But he was already pretty adept at what he was doing.

His routine included reading the newspaper in the morning before going to work. When he got back home, he would spend his time with his family. He enjoyed his life and dreamed of how he would be able to watch TV all day long when he retired at fifty.

Now, at sixty, he has been spending a lot of time watching TV shows, but he does not feel quite fulfilled with his life. He thinks how good his life would be if only he could still be as shrewd as he'd been when he was young. "Alas, it is just my brain is getting older. I can't do much about it," he's convinced himself.

His friend, Johnny, does not seem to have much of a problem with his memory, despite being the same age as Jack. Johnny has now retired, too, but his life is filled with joy. In his sixties, he is still learning Spanish, as he has been doing since his youth, without problems. He often travels to Spain to eat free *tapas* and walk the trails along the Camino de Santiago. When his grandchildren come to visit him, he enjoys using his violin to play "*Ievan Polkka*" for them.

Jack was no less accomplished than Johnny was when he was young. What did Johnny do differently than Jack did? Johnny's lifelong learning has helped him to preserve his brain function, and he can continue to improve it even at his old age. After retirement, he does not stop learning. Jack, however, does not realize that he has let his brain wither away with age by staying away from any mentally demanding activities.

This is the reality for most aging people. They follow the same aging routine as Jack has when they retire. Some may be unlucky enough to get brain diseases because of their declining brain function. In fact, there are around fifty million people with dementia worldwide, and this number is increasing by ten million new cases every year.[1]

In my years of attempting to maximize productivity, I experimented with the best ways to cultivate our brain to reap its full potential. Nothing comes close to enhancing productivity more than solid brainpower. I tested methods to learn even more with the goal of amassing more knowledge, banishing worry, and keeping my mind sharp for life. Our brains are the CEOs of our lives, and yet not many people take the effort to harness their brain's full potential.

It should be noted that I'm not, by any extent, a man with high intelligence. I just exploit the science of the brain and make it work to suit my learning objectives. This book outlines the best techniques I have accumulated throughout my lifelong learning. It not only discusses how to maintain good brain function but also lays out steps to maximize that function and use it to your advantage in the best possible way at any stage of your life. We will uncover the science behind learning, and we'll use that information to tweak some controllable variables to make it possible to learn with high rates of retention and to create a buffer against degenerative brain diseases.

Let's embark on a journey to make your brain sharper, anxiety-free, and better with time.

1

NEUROPLASTICITY

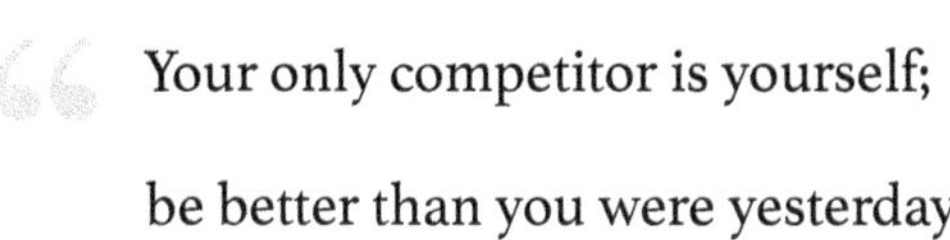

> Your only competitor is yourself;
>
> be better than you were yesterday.

Your brain is morphing every moment. It reshapes due to sensory inputs—sight, touch, hearing, taste, smell—and feelings it receives. The experiences and stimuli you give to your brain determine if it grows into a better or worse version. This phenomenon is called neuroplasticity: "neuro" referring to nerve cells in the brain and "plasticity" meaning the ability to change. Any activity you experience forms new connections with your brain cells (neurons). When you repeat an activity, your neuronal connections get stronger and become more efficient at redoing the activity. The activity becomes part of your life and easier to do. For example, if you use your left hand to write frequently, your brain will rewire and favor your left hand.

In this chapter, we will look into the triggers of neuroplasticity, the plasticity rate across different ages, and the common stimuli that alter our brains negatively.

What Is Neuroplasticity?

The concept of neuroplasticity presents both good news and bad news. The good news is that feeding your brain with positive stimuli makes it better and sharper, and the bad news is that feeding your brain with negative stimuli makes it worse and dull. Not feeding it with any stimuli at all declines its function as you age. This leaves you with just one choice—that is, to exercise your brain if you want your brain to prosper and get better with the passage of time.

Scientists long believed that the human brain stops growing after early childhood, which gave birth to a notion that you were born with a fixed IQ and ability and that there was nothing much you could do about that. At school, if your teachers deemed you a low performer, you were a low performer, and there was no use for you to even try to improve.

In 1793, however, an anatomist, Michele Vicenzo Malacarne, made the greatest discovery of humanity: the brain evolves even past childhood and until your last breath. This breakthrough gave hope to billions of children and adults who were labeled *stupid*. We know how discouraging that had to have been for them; it could bring a child's motivation to learn anything to a halt. Anyone who was made to believe that they are *stupid* can now take charge of their lives by reshaping their brains. On the other hand, anyone who believes they were born smart and stops sharpening their brains will experience a drop in brain functions as they age.

Let's look at an example: Ben Underwood has been blind since the age of three. He learned to interpret the echo that bounced back from a clicking sound from his mouth. The air current of the echo allowed him to sense nearby objects. After losing his vision, he learned this alternative way to *see*. With frequent practice, his brain remapped itself to strengthen its touch processing area, allowing him to do this even during a bike ride.

Neuroplasticity is competitive. When you exercise a certain skill, your brain maps and sharpens its connection to that skill. At the same time, it weakens the rest of the skill maps that you've stopped exercising. Over time, the skills that you don't use disappear from your system. As you stop practicing piano for a very long time, for instance, your brain gradually remaps to weaken the skill. You become what you do daily.

No one shares the same brain, for everyone has a unique experience. There are about a hundred billion neurons in your brain, and each of them can form a thousand to ten thousand connections with other neurons based on the experiences and stimuli received. This makes you uniquely you because no one can encounter the same exact experience as others do in their lifetimes.

Neural change is plastic and not elastic. Your brain will not reshape into its previous state even if you stop your current stimulation. When you have given a stimulus to your brain long enough, it becomes harder to train your brain with another stimulus. The brain always resorts to the path of least resistance, doing what you have mostly done. Therefore, encouraging a drug addict to gradually cut down his consumption only restrengthens the current neural pathway and makes the addiction grow stronger.

What Triggers Neuroplasticity?

Neuroplasticity occurs when you fulfill the following conditions:

1. Intense concentration or emotional feeling

When you are learning any new skill, you need to focus intensely. This process induces neuroplasticity. Don't confuse this with what you do at work. At the workplace, you are mostly just replaying what you already know. The learning, if any, is not as intense as what you experienced when learning trigonometry in high school. The same applies to negative experiences, such as worrying. When you always worry intensely, you are shaping your brain to be a worrier.

2. More than one neuron being activated

Neuroscientists use the phrase "neurons that fire together wire together." Any experience that fires multiple neurons at the same time makes the neuronal connection stronger. For example, say your ex-fiancée ended your relationship when the song "*Yesterday*" by *the Beatles* was playing in the background.

You were heartbroken (***intense emotional feeling***) while listening to "*Yesterday*" (***more than one neuron activated***). Your brain triggered a plastic change and associated that particular song with a terrible breakup. Long after you have moved on with your life, whenever you listen to that song, you feel sadness.

CONVERSELY, scientists have also concluded that neurons that fire apart wire apart. When neuroplasticity occurs, the connection it forms with the fired neurons is strengthened. At the same time, the connections it used to have with other neurons that are not fired are weakened. Repeatedly firing these neurons together makes the connections sturdy, while it recedes non-associated connections. This gives you a way to unlearn negative connections your brain has formed earlier.

Consider the breakup example. Your brain has associated "Yesterday" with a terrible breakup. To unlearn this association, you can help your brain form a new connection by either:

- Linking "*Yesterday*" with happiness, or
- Linking another song with a terrible breakup

Certainly, the former is preferred, for it would be awful to experience another terrible breakup just to help your brain reshape. Setting up this change is not easy. You have attempted to stay away from the song "*Yesterday*" forever. Whenever it played on the radio, you would switch the channel; whenever your roommate played that song, you would try to go out.

If you want your brain to unlearn this, you need to face the song again, but you must do so with the intense opposite emotion. Whenever you experience happiness, deliberately play that song again. This is not always practical. You don't carry around your music player just to catch every unpredictable moment of happiness. But if you can successfully set this up enough, you can help your brain unlearn the negative association.

Thus, to maximize your brain plasticity, you want to help your brain ***strengthen*** its connections with the neurons that store desired knowledge, attitudes, and habits, and ***weaken*** its connections with the neurons that store those that are undesired.

Plasticity Fluctuation

The plasticity of the brain does not stay constant throughout your lifespan.

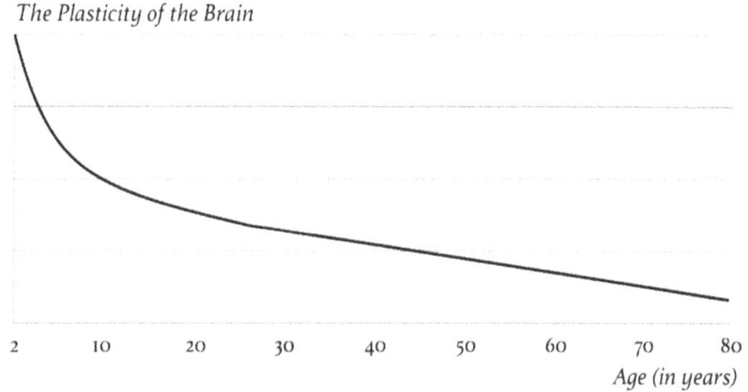

The Plasticity of the Brain Throughout a Human Lifespan

Source: Levitt (2009)

Neuroplasticity peaks between the ages of one and two. Infants' brains are extremely plastic. Their learning capacity is at its best, and they can pick up language and sound easily. Biologically, this is an important gift since it allows humans to adapt to the world from the very start of their lives.

During this period, it's critical to make sure an infant is well taken care of and exposed to an enriching environment. Any environmental problems that bring negative impacts to the child, such as repetitive abuse or the death of their parents, could form long-lasting alterations in their brain's circuitry, unless a deliberate effort is made to rewire their brain. Most mental disorders in adults can be traced back to their childhood or infancy period.[1]

As you get older, your brain becomes more resistant to change. It is still possible to change it, but you need to exert greater effort to do so.

Science has discovered there is another period when neuroplasticity occurs as rapidly as it did during the infant stage. This happens when you fall in love with someone. During this period, your brain releases oxytocin, also called the love hormone. It is released when people bond in a relationship.

The emotion created is incredibly powerful (***intense concentration***), and your brain's reward center surges when you love someone (***multiple neurons fire together***), enabling your brain to rewire massively. Researchers analyzed the brains of people who fell in love and discovered that the reward system activation in their brains looked similar to that in people who were addicted to cocaine.[2]

Falling in love is a beautiful thing for both your mind and your brain. You begin to view the world beautifully, and you are full of optimism. Rigid personality traits often can be changed during this period. You attempt to integrate your lover's life into yours. You remember your lover's perfume's smell, their behavior, favorite food, and many other things. It is not surprising that some lovers turn out to be better people than who they were before. Some people like to call it the power of love. Now, you can call it the power of neuroplasticity.

The reverse applies, too. When you enter into a bad romantic relationship, you rewire your brain negatively if you cannot overcome your emotions. The negative emotions involved can turn you into an anxious person, a pessimistic person, or a depressed person.

There are some interesting indicators that point toward massive plasticity during parenthood too, but it is inconclusive.[3] Further study will be needed to confirm this.

As children grow into adults, any unused or rarely used neuronal connections die away—what scientists call synaptic pruning. This process continues to last for the rest of a person's life after adolescence. The part of the brain called the hippocampus is responsible for stripping off infrequently used neurons in order to make room for the frequently used neurons and allow the latter to be stored in long-term memory and called upon more efficiently.

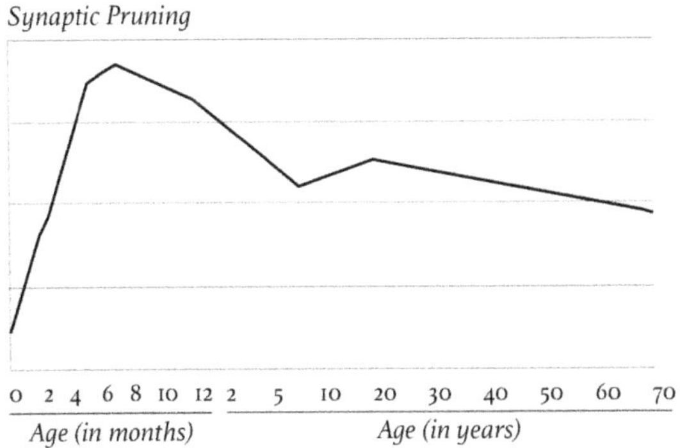

Synaptic Pruning

Source: Huttenlocher (1994)

Pruning is necessary to allow your brain to be more efficient at learning new things. During infancy, the peaking of neuronal connections is pivotal for infants to learn everything. As they grow older, the connections must be trimmed so they can discriminate what to learn and what not to learn.

Modern Life's Influence

Our modern lifestyle brings about several influences when it comes to reshaping our brains. We will cover the most prominent ones.

Television

On average, people worldwide spend close to three hours per day watching television. TV is an invention that rewires your brain in many ways. In a real world, the "scenes" you see and hear transition slowly, unless there is a sudden noise or someone startles you from behind, which does not happen often. Your brain has time to orient itself when you walk to another street or room (enter a new scene). What you see on TV, however, happens too fast. Moviemakers cut unwanted scenes, combine many scenes, and zoom in and out of scenes when necessary to make movies interesting. Even a live show is recorded with multiple cameras and shown on TV from different viewpoints.

All of these cause your brain to reorient itself many times in a span of a minute. Your brain is overstimulated by this fast-paced experience, which otherwise would be impossible to get without TV—except when you are riding a roller coaster. We like to think that it's a good thing that everything is instant, but over time, our brain rewires to expect everything at high speed. You will have difficulty focusing on one thing at a time. When you are talking to someone, your brain is quick to wonder and crave for other *scenes*. Whenever you are doing something, your brain soon becomes hungry for another *scene*.

Activities that demand sustained attention, such as reading books, become more challenging. They are boring because the pace is too slow and they lack sensory stimulation compared to the rapidity and multi-sensory experience that TV offers.

Research on over two thousand preschool children in 2019 found that children who spent over two hours on screens per day were 7.7 times more likely to develop attention deficit hyperactivity disorder.[4] Frequent screen time alters the brain to expect fast scene changes; however, it remains uncertain if ADHD was directly caused by the structural change of the brain from watching TV alone or by the lack of other activities the children missed out on in favor of watching.

Regardless of what the reason may be, it is best to avoid binge watching and cut down your screen time to the minimum. Besides, a study of 3,662 adults over the age of fifty suggested that watching TV for over three and a half hours a day impaired verbal memory by 8 to 10 percent in the next six years.[5] Among those who watched less than three and a half hours a day, the impairment of verbal memory was only 4 to 5 percent. This was a controlled study in which the result was not dependent on the participants' physical health, depression or lack thereof, or other health problems.

Internet

The Internet gives us a lot of benefits. The massive information that travels at lightning speed; the Google search that presents you an answer almost instantly; the infinite background songs you can stream; the different web page orientations. All these distractions reduce the opportunity for you to pause and think deeply. Your brain craves more new information that you can access from your web browser within a blink of an eye. Your brain is accustomed to demand rapid-fire information filled with rich stimulations. It learns to skim and filter out only what you want from the sea of text, advertisements, and animated objects.

When you navigate the Web, you constantly inundate your working memory by switching your attention frequently and making many rapid decisions in the process. You want to get the information as fast as your eyes can read and your fingers can move. This taxes your mental resources, obstructing your higher-order thinking, and makes you prone to misinterpreting crucial information. The Internet draws your intense attention only to deliver you more competing distractions. The more you feed this to your brain, the more you indulge it.

The same effect that you get from watching TV too much can come from the Internet, too. Watching TV is a passive activity, but browsing the Internet is an active activity that stimulates all of your sensory inputs except taste and smell, making it a perfect medium for neuroplasticity.

1. **Sight:** skimming fast information
2. **Touch:** typing on the keyboard, scrolling the mouse up and down, closing pop-up notifications
3. **Hearing:** *ding* sounds during error notifications

There is no denying that the Internet has altered the human experience of processing information. As of October 2020, there are 4.66 billion active Internet users.[6] While this technology improves human life tremendously, the negative effect it causes to our brains cannot be ignored. We have learned that neuroplasticity is competitive, what we use is strengthened, and what we don't use is weakened.

- We have strengthened our brain's capacity to skim information but have weakened its capacity for linear thinking. Composing long paragraphs becomes an intricate task.
- We have strengthened our brain's capacity to filter a large amount of text but have weakened its capacity to focus. Paying full attention while listening to your spouse becomes increasingly difficult.
- We have strengthened our brain's capacity to expect speedy responses but have weakened its capacity to immerse in deep reading. Leafing static pages of books to learn new things becomes a mundane and irritating task.

Neuroplasticity causes your brain to behave in a similar way, even when you are away from the Internet. The change of behavior is not conspicuous for most of us as it has become ingrained into our lives. If you have tried any long period of digital detox, such as spending a vacation in a rural village without an Internet connection, you would notice the difference in pacing as you start to use the Internet again.

Many people believe that the ability to scan tons of information makes them smarter and more efficient compared to if they took the time to read two hundred-page books. There is no reason to read books when Google can give you the answer in one second. The trade-off of becoming impatient readers is justifiable to them.

People have also increased their reliance on Google for information outsourcing. Gone are the days when people needed to remember many facts to keep up with their lives. A study in 2011 showed that people are not apt to remember any information if they believe it is just a Google search away.[7] This phenomenon is called the *Google Effect*. "Why bother to remember a piece of information when you can just Google it?" most people would retort. By and large, this holds true; instead of setting up your brain as a warehouse of facts, you would be better off reserving its resources for creative thinking. But allowing Google to be the be-all and end-all for your learning, instead of having it as just a supplementary means, reduces your time spent on critical thinking. As you repeatedly train your brain to rely on a search engine for data retrieval, you induce plasticity in your brain and atrophy its memorizing function.

Because of its ease of accessibility and necessity in most jobs, the Internet is arguably the most mind-altering technology in this era. It is not inherently good or bad. We are now living in a time when we have to accept the loss of concentration, focus, and memory in exchange for a wealth of speedy information that the Internet offers.

Pornography

Forty million adults in the U.S. watch online pornography regularly. Watching pornography quickly floods your brain with dopamine. Dopamine is a reward system that is activated in your brain when you experience pleasurable activity or achieve your goals. Combining the ***intense concentration*** with support from the reward system (***more than one neuron activated***) makes this a strong recipe for neuroplasticity to occur. And because it involves dopamine in the process, this can lead to addiction without you even being aware of it. As you crave and watch more, your brain rewires in multiple ways, causing the following:

1. Erectile dysfunction

When you liberally and repeatedly watch erotic scenes, one after another, your tolerance level builds up. You need more and more substance from the pornographic scenes to gain the pleasure. Your spouse, who you still consider attractive, no longer turns you on as your brain acquires new sexual preferences. Excessive addiction to porn alters your perception of sex and induces erectile dysfunction. Even though erectile dysfunction can arise from medical issues, too, the pornographic epidemic is likely the profound cause. Researchers conducted a survey on over three thousand men on their porn habit.[8] They found a high correlation between the hours spent watching porn and erectile dysfunction.

2. Aggressive personality

Pornography can make your personality more aggressive toward your spouse. There are varieties of porn types, including one that projects aggressive scenes. Watching that type of video repeatedly rewires your brain to gain a new sexual taste and associate pain with pleasure. To fulfill your sexual desire, you crave supplementing it with sexual assault. Having sex is no longer the act of making love but a platform to express dominance and aggression.

In the era of the Internet, it is difficult to avoid pornography. If we are not careful, our children, who have very plastic brains, can be exposed to pornography easily. It lurks just about everywhere, from links in ads to scam emails.

Addiction to pornography can cause a lifelong change to your brain. Total abstinence is the only way to recover until your brain rewires into normality. Let your brain gradually weaken the connections it has built with problematic neurons.

Social Media

As of 2020, over 3.6 billion people worldwide use social media.[9] One of the prominent uses of social media is to collect "likes" of each posting. For each "like" earned, your brain's reward system releases dopamine. You get a fleeting happy feeling and are motivated to get more. Similar to how drugs affect your nervous system, your tolerance level increases. Soon, a single "like" or tens of "likes" is no longer appealing to you, and you crave even more "likes."

In the past, gaining the public's "likes" required a tremendous amount of hard work. Perhaps your art won an award, your music hit the billboard list, or you won an acting audition. Now, you can get the same feeling just by posting photos. Continuing to do this to garner more "likes" rewires your brain to associate more "likes" with happiness. Your source of motivation becomes the social media "likes," and getting more of them makes you proud. When you don't have enough "likes," or someone "dislikes" your posts, you feel anxious or devastated.

It is undeniable that social media is a prominent marketing platform to gain a following; however, uncontrolled time spent on social media sacrifices a lot of creative time. Studies show that talking about yourself increases dopamine. Social media enables you not only to collect "likes" but also to show off your life, making it a highly addictive combo. Your brain rewires and knows that it is easier to get dopamine highs through social media instead of working hard toward accomplishing your goals.

Social media grabs a lot of attention from you—often more than the person sitting next to you. It feels more rewarding to attend to someone who has just praised your post than to ask your parents if they had a good day. The ability to post updates and broadcast thoughts can sometimes generate anxiety to social media users. The phenomenon of fear of missing out, or FOMO, is particularly risky for teenagers who are prone to be compulsive social media users. When they stop using it, they feel the anxiety of not being kept updated and fear becoming invisible to others.

Similar to the effect of the Internet, social media reinforces your brain's craving for more—often unrelated—information. You are training your brain to get distracted and overloaded with information. You want more distraction, and you refuse moments of calmness. When you are away from your phone, you are hungry to check out if there is any new post, reply, or email.

The instant messaging feature of social media is widely used alongside work in the name of achieving a meritorious multitasking ability and high productivity. This hijacks your attention further and amplifies your brain's craving to be overwhelmed with distractions. The more you multitask, the less deliberative you are. You sacrifice mindful knowledge acquisition and deep processing. You can continue to train your brain to multitask and still deliver something, but you will never be as good as if you just focused on one thing at a time.

Social media is dominating our lives today, even for young children. If you are not careful, you could feed your children with this *digital drug*.

Video Games

When we want to feel better, we turn to the activities that can release the most dopamine. Video games are one of the easiest ways to get a large number of dopamine hits, one that is comparable to taking an addictive substance.[10] It is a drug in disguise.

The reward that you can get from a video game encourages you to continue playing. Instead of building up yourself, you are partial to building up your virtual character in the video game. You tend to neglect your health, hygiene, relationships, and work in favor of your nonexistent life in the game. Real life seems to lack stimulation compared to the high stakes and jam-packed action in video games. We won't delve into the psychological impact of this, or how it can cause your grades in school to suffer, but we will look into the problem it causes in the brain.

The brain's highest involvement in playing video games is vision and movement control. A dopamine release, coupled with intense concentration, makes video games a trigger for neuroplasticity. Playing one for hours in a long run rewires your brain to under-develop other regions of the brain that govern your behavior, learning, and emotions.

Playing violent games also rewards aggressive tendencies. The problem is exacerbated if you also possess an aggressive personality.

Video game developers have long learned to make games as addictive as possible. They include the right components to activate your reward system and feed your impulsive behavior to keep you playing forever. A gradual increase of difficulty continues to fuel your desire to beat a game. Small rewards with occasional big rewards are introduced to release your dopamine. The sound effects after beating an enemy, collecting a reward, and increasing your character level immerse you into the game and enhance your feeling of achievement.

Young children are often exposed to video games in the name of early education or simply as an entertainment treat. What parents don't realize is the problems it causes in their children's brains. Because of the flood of dopamine experienced, removing video games from their lives triggers withdrawal symptoms and intense cravings. Consequently, video games lead to addiction. As with other dopamine-flooding addictions, quitting video games requires that you go cold turkey. Otherwise, you will only reinforce your addiction.

SUFFICE TO SAY, your brain reshapes every day through your culture, your environment, and your habits. Feed your brain with positive behavior, and it grows into a brain with positive behavior. Feed it with negativity, and it grows into a negative brain. It is much easier to influence a child's brain, while it is still very plastic.

When you exercise your brain in the direction you want to go frequently, you strengthen it. If you wish to be an efficient learner but you rarely engage in deep learning, your brain does not know how to learn efficiently.

The sooner you form positive plasticity in your brain, the sooner and longer you will enjoy the fruition. It is easier for most people to lean toward negative stimuli because they are quick to release dopamine. The brain rewires fast when the pleasure system, dopamine, is activated, which further reinforces the repetition of activities. Positive stimuli such as studying or learning art simply do not produce dopamine as fast as the negative ones. Thus, it is easy to lean toward the negative ones if you are not careful. Once your brain has established negative behavior for a long time, it can be very hard to reverse this with positive behavior.

Next, we will look into the building blocks of brain cells, what decreases and increases your number of brain cells, and how to keep them from dying.

2

NEUROGENESIS

> Happy people build their inner world; unhappy people blame their outer world.
>
> — T. Harv Eker

Neuroplasticity makes use of existing brain cells, also known as neurons, to form connections. Existing neurons die off when not in use for a long time. If you want to enrich your brain with more connections to learn more or increase your cognitive function, you need to increase the neuron count in your brain. The process of generating new neurons is called ***neurogenesis***.

Problems with a Low Neuron Count

Your brain releases brain-derived neurotrophic factor, or BDNF, when multiple neurons fire together to help increase neurogenesis and speed up your brain's ability to affect plasticity. BDNF connects the associated neurons together and makes them likely to fire together again the next time one of them is fired. A high amount of BDNF also increases the survival rate of neurons. Every time new neurons are created, only about 30-40 percent of them survive under normal circumstances. Without putting in any effort to grow more neurons, the existing neurons steadily decrease. You lose approximately fifty thousand neurons every day out of the total hundred billion neurons. As you age, millions of neurons die naturally, which commonly leads to age-related mental decline. Those who get neurodegenerative diseases, such as Alzheimer's disease, dementia, and Parkinson's disease, experience a further speeding up of neuronal cell death. It makes sense to work toward increasing your neuron count as early as possible to enjoy the benefits sooner and longer.

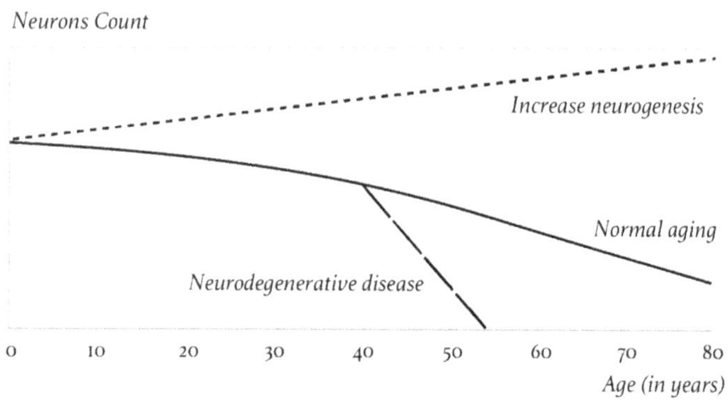

Neuron Loss by Normal Aging vs. Neurodegenerative Disease

Having a low number of neurons causes the following problems:

- Memory loss
- Brain shrinkage
- Increased vulnerability to stress and anxiety
- Lowered immunity
- Lowered cognitive functions
- Depression
- Dementia

Having a lacking brain capacity takes a big toll on a person's life. To patients with dementia, the world seems to have ended. They continually challenge the patience of their caregivers through their repetitive forgetfulness, exhibit troubling behavior occasionally, and worry their family members when they wander out of the house. They are sometimes seen as objects of laughter by their grandchildren. Unlike some who have passed away before their brain deteriorated to this condition, these patients need to struggle until their last breath.

The major stages of dementia include:

1. Normal mental decline during aging

You look outwardly fine. There is no noticeable sign of dementia that affects your work. From time to time, you forget things. You notice that you are no longer as sharp as you were during your youth.

2. Mild cognitive impairment

At this stage, your memory loss increases rapidly. The quality of your life drops dramatically. You frequently forget things, have trouble concentrating, are more fearful, get lost more frequently, and ask repetitive questions. Carrying out your routine becomes overwhelming. With no effort taken to prevent further loss of memory, you will progress to the early stage of dementia after two to seven years.

3. Dementia (early stage and beyond)

When you have reached this stage, the damage to your brain is already beyond repair. The decline has sped up so swiftly that stopping further damage is difficult. You need help for most activities, forget names, suffer from urinary incontinence, and undergo personality and emotional changes. You will progress to the end stage of dementia within seven or eight years, when you cannot speak or walk anymore. Stopping the damage from snowballing into dementia before this early stage is the only solution to escape the problem.

It has been found that to have healthy, enhanced mental abilities and a well-functioning brain in your old age, you must increase the number of neurons in your brain. Unlike what was previously believed, cognitive decline is preventable, and it is possible for human brains to continue to generate new neurons even in old age. This can be achieved by:

- Increasing the rate of neuron generation (neurogenesis), and
- Reducing the number of dying neurons (neurodegeneration)

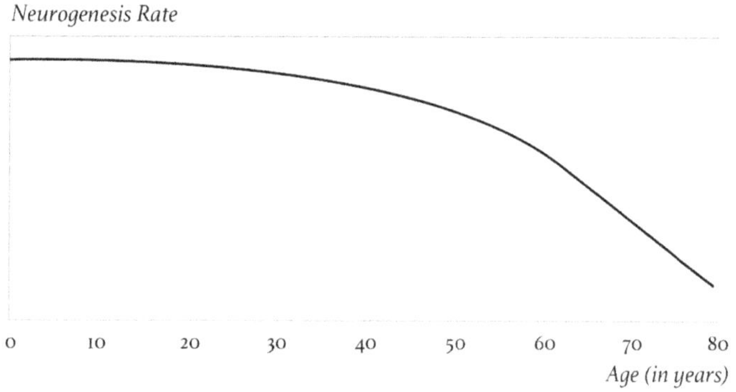

Neurogenesis Rate by Age

Neurogenesis rate begins to slow by age thirty, and then further slows in older age. On average, mental decline is already noticeable between age forty and age sixty. Without any interception to improve your neurogenesis after age thirty, the risk of developing a mental illness increases with age, as the neurogenesis rate is faster at a younger age than it is at an older age. The younger you are when you start to actively take care of your brain, the longer you get to enjoy its benefits throughout your lifespan. The longer you wait to take any action, the more neurons die, and the more time it will take to regenerate the neurons to an optimal level. If you decide to tackle this earlier in your life, you will enjoy compounded benefits of what your brain can give you.

However, don't be discouraged; it is never too late to do anything about it. Start now by feeding your brain with the right stimulations.

Factors That Decrease Your Neurogenesis Rate

The rate of the neuron generation differs from person to person. Your lifestyle and environment affect the rate of neurogenesis. Let's look at the factors that ***decrease*** neurogenesis. Some of these may be out of your control, but there are a few things that you can control to reduce neurodegeneration.

Loneliness

Being alone reduces neurogenesis and BDNF by a significant amount. Neuroscientists performed a study on two groups of twenty rats: in one group, each rat lived alone in an isolated cage; and in the other, each rat lived together with another random rat. After fourteen days, the neurogenesis rate of the isolated group was lowered by 95 percent compared to the socialized group.[1] Not only did their neurogenesis rate decline, but their working memory also slowed down by 37 percent compared to the socialized group. There is no direct measurement that can be confirmed in a human brain. However, we can rely on the findings in these rat tests because rats' genetics and behavioral characteristics resemble those of humans. Many of the medical problems in humans can be replicated in rats.

Research has also shown that people who feel lonely have a shorter lifespan.[2] Therefore, never let your aging parents live alone. It is possible to restore your neurogenesis rate by re-engaging in social life, even though the potential for increasing the neurogenesis during the lonely period is already lost.[3]

Stress

One of the few leading causes of neurogenesis decline is stressful experiences. Temporary stress, such as that induced by strenuous exercising followed by a recovery, is fine. The problem is chronic stress, when the stressful experience is prolonged with insufficient recovery time. During chronic stress, your body is in the constant state of alertness and assiduously recruits resources to mount a defense, even when no danger is present. Chronic stress not only reduces neurogenesis rate and BDNF but also kills existing neurons, with newly formed neurons being the most susceptible.[4] It causes manifold other adverse effects to your health, too.

Stressful experiences manifest in many forms. We will look into major stresses that blunt neurogenesis rate, including:

1. Poor relationships

Scientists have shown that good relationships with other human beings increase neurogenesis, but poor relationships bring neurogenesis to a halt or even kill existing neurons. It is important to avoid toxic relationships, not only to save you from mental stress but also to maintain a high neurogenesis rate.

A one-time stressful relationship experience will not affect your neurogenesis rate much, but staying in a stressful relationship for long decreases your neurons. A few examples are as follows:

- Working a stressful job
- Living with abusive parents
- Having to sit next to a bullying classmate
- Marrying a demeaning partner

2. Insecurity

Living in an unstable position induces a lot of stress and is harmful to neurogenesis. Immigrants face a lot of uncertainty and constantly worry about whether they can gain permanent residency in an unfamiliar country; concentration camp prisoners do not know when their imprisonment will be over; job seekers who always change jobs live lives that lack fiscal stability.

WE ARE BOUND to face many stressors in life. Stress lowers your neurogenesis rate; a lower neurogenesis rate lowers your resistance to stress. Chronic stress can spiral the problem out of control if it is not overcome.

CAFFEINE

A STUDY in 2007 suggested that the long-term consumption of caffeine, even as low as 0.3 mg/kg, reduces neurogenesis.[5] This is equivalent to less than a quarter cup of coffee for someone who weighs fifty kilograms.

It may be hard to believe because when you drink a cup of coffee, your heightened mental state and alertness do not make you feel like your brain cell generation is reducing. This is an important issue for most people because coffee is the most-drunk beverage in the world after water.

Coffee is indeed a powerful substance that helps you gain a temporary jolt of energy. Given its negative impact on your neurogenesis rate, however, only use it during critical moments such as before taking an exam. If drinking one cup will reduce your neurogenesis rate, make each cup count. But if you don't drink caffeinated drinks, don't introduce any into your routine.

Alcohol

Alcohol is another offender when it comes to a decline in your neurogenesis rate. In 2012, scientists experimented by feeding a moderate amount of alcohol to rats for two weeks.[6] The study did not find any sensory, motor, or learning impairment in the rats, but it did find a 40 percent reduction in their neurogenesis rates. That is an enormous amount of potential neuron growth wasted. Chronic drinkers and adolescents who binge drink three to four alcoholic beverages per day risk decreased neurogenesis rates.

Inflammation

Any food that causes inflammation reduces neurogenesis and BDNF.[7] The following are the most inflammatory foods that you should avoid or cut down on if you wish to have a high neurogenesis rate:

1. **Sugar.** Having a high sugar level is associated with cognitive decline.
2. **Artificial sweeteners.** These are regularly present in soda and fruit juice.
3. **Trans fat.** Margarine, donuts, and processed food contain trans fat. It not only raises your bad cholesterol level (LDL) but also increases your risk of Alzheimer's.
4. **Refined carbs.** The primary sources of this are flour, pasta, cereal, and white bread. Refined carbs reduce BDNF in your brain.[8]

These ingredients are often found in fast food. The excess body fat these foods cause also leads to neurogenesis decline. You become what you eat.

Research found that about 34 percent of children and teenagers between the ages of two and nineteen eat fast food on any given day.[9] Just as it is possible to acquire a new sexual taste from pornographic exploitation, it is possible to acquire a taste for foods that you consume frequently. Children whose neuroplasticity is still heightened are at a higher risk of acquiring a new taste for fast food.

Mercury

Even a small amount of mercury kills brain cells.[10] Sadly, almost all seafood contains traces of mercury, although it is a good source of Omega-3 fatty acids and high-quality protein.

Coal burning, forest burning, gold mining, industrial wastage, and metal production are major sources of mercury contamination in the oceans. Large and long-lived fish have a higher concentration of mercury because they are exposed to mercury the most.

	Mercury amount per kg (in mg)
King mackerel	0.73
Lobster	0.15
Canned tuna	0.12
Stingray	0.11
Cod	0.09
Salmon	0.06
Crab	0.06
Sardine	0.02
Anchovies	0.01

Common Seafood with Their Mercury Content

Young children whose brains are still developing are especially prone to brain damage from mercury-laden food consumption. Aim to minimize eating seafood with mercury concentration that is greater than 0.1 mg/kg.

Noise Pollution

Traffic noise, construction site noise, airport noise, and industrial noise have been shown to decrease neurogenesis. A study observed that children living near a noisy airport or highway have meager cognitive performance.[11] Continuous exposure to noise causes long-term reduction in neurogenesis.[12] Usually the noise pollution goes unnoticed because it has become a background noise, especially if you live in the same place for a long time. If you live at a place that is exposed to constant noise pollution, setting up some noise insulation can alleviate the problem.

Under-Stimulation

Living a life lacking in stimulation reduces neurogenesis. For example, bed-ridden patients whose only activity is watching TV or prisoners who are confined in a cell experience this. Retired elderlies who live alone are prone to follow the same dull routine every day. A stagnant environment declines neurogenesis significantly. Many people surrender their lives to what their environment dictates; therefore, they end up worse than they were before.

When trapped in an under-stimulated environment, you can still work on stimulating your brain instead of letting it rot. Consider Chris Wilson, who was imprisoned at the age of seventeen and charged with murder. He received a lifetime sentence in prison. One would easily feel hopeless and give up on anything, but not him. With the luxury of time, he read, wrote, and learned four languages while he was behind bars. These activities kept his neurogenesis strong. After sixteen years, the judge released him from prison. He is now the owner of multiple companies, including the Barclay Investment Corporation.

Given the non-stimulating environment of prisons, only a small number of inmates are self-motivated enough to follow the path of Chris Wilson and get out of prison as better people. Surely, without understanding the degrading impact to the brain, one would not be eager to work on any stimulating activities. The longer inmates stay imprisoned, the longer their neurogenesis suffers. Finland implemented an open prison concept that does not lock prisoners inside gates. The inmates have Internet access to take online courses and are allowed to study for degrees. This enriching environment supports inmates' brain development.

Children who live in orphanages and are bereft of stimulating facilities face a bigger problem because their brains are still highly malleable. Studies show that their cognitive function is delayed badly, and some develop autism.[13]

Now that we have covered the factors that contribute to lowering neurogenesis rates, let's go through what helps to increase the neurogenesis rate and BDNF.

Factors That Increase Neurogenesis Rates

Intuitively, any activity that increases neurogenesis is also one that makes us feel better.

Education

Education is an amazing way to sharpen your brain, and the result it brings can be life changing. There is nothing like continuous learning that causes radical improvement in neurogenesis rate. Effortful thinking shapes your brain to think better. Studies show that education increases neurons, contributing significantly to thicker brain tissue.[14] This gives you a lot of buffers against neurodegenerative diseases. Some studies suggest that less education is associated with a greater risk of dementia, even though the result is inconsistent among different study populations.[15]

In order to continuously stimulate your brain to maximize its neurogenesis, you must strive to always learn something new. Neurogenesis thrives best when you expend effort on learning new things, even though it is understandably deterring for most to learn something unfamiliar.

There is a multitude of ways to learn something new. Try attending new courses, teaching others, pursuing a higher education degree, or reading different books. Learning a new language, for example, is one way to strengthen your brain and make neural pathways more efficient. Studies show that new language acquisition causes brain changes, regardless of age.[16] Language learning is an intensive type of training. The effort and focus needed to remember every unfamiliar new word makes it a cognitively demanding activity. Learning new languages also increases the gray and white matter density in the brain. This intense concentration forms the bedrock for neuroplasticity to occur.

Note: Gray matter is the neural tissue that covers many regions of the brain that handle muscle coordination, memory formation, and emotions. White matter connects all the gray matter. Together, they foster stronger and more efficient neural connections in the brain.

Even though you may be past school life, cultivating a habit of daily learning maintains a well-functioning brain and gives you a higher satisfaction in life. Remember that plasticity is competitive; learning something new can rewire millions of connections in our existing brain cells, while weakening connections that are not in use. Thus, you want to make sure what you learn benefits you or at least makes you happy.

Fasting

A study done on mice showed that not eating for at least twelve hours increases neurogenesis and BDNF.[17] Further increasing the fasting period to sixteen hours increases neurogenesis even more.

During the period of fasting, your body starts its repairing process and increases neurogenesis. There are many other benefits of intermittent fasting, which I won't cover here. I recommend practicing daily time-restricted fasting to set your body's clock in synchronicity with your eating time and improve your overall well-being.

Physical Exercise

Researchers found that not all exercises affect neurogenesis and BDNF.

- Anaerobic exercise does not increase neurogenesis or BDNF[18], while aerobic exercise increases both neurogenesis and BDNF.
- Intense aerobic exercise and anaerobic exercise[19] increase BDNF the most.

Note: Aerobic exercise uses the continuous supply of oxygen to sustain the workout. Examples of aerobic exercise are jogging, cycling, and swimming. Anaerobic exercise requires a higher amount of oxygen than aerobic exercise does. During a shortage of oxygen, your body uses glycogen from muscle cells as fuel to withstand the exercise. Examples of anaerobic exercise are strength training and sprinting.

Researchers compared two groups of mice: one group with an exercise wheel in the cage and another group without one. The mice with the exercise wheels ran on the wheel daily. After a month, their brain examinations showed that the mice that exercised roughly doubled their neurons in quantity, compared to the mice that did not have any exercise facility in the cage.[20]

There are countless other benefits that exercise offers. If you want to have a strong and healthy brain, physical exercise is a non-negotiable activity that you must commit to in your life.

Mental Exercise

Mental training, such as playing brain games, increases neurogenesis. To exercise your brain more strenuously, you can increase the training difficulty.

It should be noted that playing brain games does not make you smarter, as many products may claim.[21] The improvement is limited to only the game that you are playing, and it does not extend to other areas of your intelligence. To be an expert in a specific field takes an arduous amount of hard work and definitely isn't achievable by just playing a brain game. Mental games could, however, help you learn faster because of the by-products of increased focus and concentration.

Playing a musical instrument is a demanding mental exercise. It also induces neuroplasticity because of the multi-sensory experience, that is, motor actions associated with the sound feedback. Repeated practice strengthens the connections between the motor and auditory regions in the brain. Studies also show that musicians have a higher amount of gray matter in the brain.[22]

Any literacy activity, including writing, increases neurogenesis and reshapes your brain, too. The German neuroscientist Martin Lotze and his team observed increased activity in multiple brain regions during creative writing.[23] Long-term writers showed similar brain activities as that of musicians and athletes who develop complex skills.

A thorough brain stimulation requires you to exercise multiple areas of your brain by learning a variety of things: music, vocabulary, art, mathematics, problem-solving. Trying to master every ability is not possible with your limited lifespan; it is important that you pick mental activities that you enjoy.

Silence

Music INCREASES NEUROGENESIS. Most people will be happy to know that. There isn't any conclusive answer on what music work best. Therefore, enjoy the musics you like.

Natural sounds, such as a waterfall, birds' chirping, and wind gusts, promote even better neurogenesis than music does. We are built to live in nature. The vibrant colors and soothing sounds in nature provide a lot of positive stimulations to your senses. Exposing yourself to natural sounds also relieves your stress and anxiety levels, which results in an increase in neurogenesis. Living off-grid does more than just lowering your carbon footprint. It can be difficult to experience nature if you are living in a city, but you can plan for frequent visits to parks.

Silence increases neurogenesis the most.[24] It is a rare commodity and even considered uncomfortable for some.

Sleep

Scientists theorized that neurogenesis occurs mostly during sleep. Make getting sufficient sleep a priority in life. When you don't sleep enough, your neurogenesis rate reduces.[25] Prolonged sleep deprivation lasting over three days reduces the rate of neurogenesis by 30-80 percent.[26] Insufficient sleep also increases your stress, which further exacerbates neurogenesis decline.

Touch

Research suggests it is possible that touch increases neurogenesis.[27] In one study, the more touch human babies received, the higher their neurogenesis rate was when they grew up. For the touch to work, it must come from trusted sources, such as parents or even pets, because that induces an oxytocin release. Both the giver and receiver get the benefit of increased neurogenesis.

Scientists found that mice raised by two parents have higher neurogenesis rates than mice with only one parent when the mice become adults.[28] Children raised by both parents also likely receive more touch, compared to those raised by a single parent.

Increasing Your Neuron Survival Rate

We have learned earlier that only about half of newly formed neurons survive and integrate into your brain. To maximize your brain cell count, you need to increase not only the neurogenesis rate but also the survival rate of new neurons. The following factors increase the survivability of new neurons.

1. Living in an enriching environment

Living in an enriching environment increases your neuron survival rate by 80-100 percent. An enriching environment includes anything that enables learning or intellectual stimulation, such as toys, puzzles, books, painting materials, and musical instruments.

2. Eating solid food

Research performed on mice shows that soft food consumption reduced their BDNF and neuron survival rate.[29] The problem with soft food is the lack of chewing required. The action of chewing increases the survival rate of new neurons.[30] Even though the study has not been replicated on humans, it pays to ensure the majority of your food is solid and to curtail the consumption of soft food, such as fruit juice, blended food, mashed potatoes, and jelly. Elderlies are often at a higher risk of consuming a lot of soft food after losing their teeth.

3. Avoiding head trauma

A blow to a head can damage the delicate brain and kill some neurons—not just the newly formed neurons, but also the existing ones. Sports that can cause head trauma such as boxing, wrestling, and American football have a higher risk of losing neurons.[31] A study of 202 deceased American football players in 2017 discovered that 99 percent of them were diagnosed with a neurodegenerative disease that caused mood, behavioral, and thinking problems.[32] Researchers also believe that a single traumatic brain injury speeds up the risk of developing a brain disease by 56 percent in later years.[33]

4. Limiting alcohol consumption

Earlier, we learned that alcohol decreases neurogenesis. Alcohol also kills existing neurons. A test done on rats showed a neuronal cell death rate of 227-279 percent just by feeding them a moderate amount of alcohol.[34]

IMPROVING your neurogenesis rate ultimately improves your entire life because it affects how you think, act, and function. As you maintain a high number of brain cells with a high neurogenesis rate throughout your life, you also protect your brain from reaching the intermediate or late stages of memory impairment, regardless of your age. Think about the amazing things your healthy brain can do for you.

Some negative neurogenesis experiences may be inescapable in your life. You can balance them out with more positive neurogenesis activities. You may have seen some people who practice a lot of neurogenesis-reducing activities but who survive into old age without dementia. Those coffee drinkers may have happy family relationships; an employee who deals with his demeaning boss daily may be tending to his garden after work; the alcohol drinker may be an exercise junkie. The key is to have a higher proportion of positive neurogenesis experiences compared to negative ones.

3

MAXIMIZE LEARNING

> The more I learn, the more excited I get.
>
> — Johnny Cash

Learning is an integral part of maximizing neurogenesis and neuroplasticity. The more you learn, the more your brain rewires and changes its structure to improve its capacity to learn even more by increasing its perceiving and thinking speed. Not making use of this benefit is clearly a waste. In this chapter, we will discuss ways to maximize your learning journey.

Science of Memory

There are two main types of memory: ***short-term memory*** and ***long-term memory***.

You use ***short-term memory*** to hold information temporarily, and it can only hold a limited amount of information: for example, when you walk into a room and are introduced to several people. With no effort, your capability to remember all the people's names relies on your short-term memory. Short-term memory has very limited capacity to hold the information; it can hold about five to nine items for only about twenty seconds or less. To keep information in the short-term memory longer, you need to rehearse the information. Any distraction can cause you to forget the information.

On the other hand, ***long-term memory*** stores information for as long as weeks, months, years, or decades. The storage is thought to be unlimited—at least no one has ever reached its limit yet. You just need to recall if you need to access the information in this storage. Some stored memories are not easily recalled, such as your childhood events, while some of them are easy to recall, such as your phone number. The higher your neurogenesis rate, the better your memory will function to help you with the recall.

Within the short-term memory, there is a component called ***working memory***. You use the working memory to manipulate data you retrieve from short-term memory and long-term memory. The memory comes into your awareness only after you retrieve it from your long-term memory or short-term memory to your working memory. If you are asked to calculate 25 x 20, your working memory will draw upon both short-term memory and long-term memory to produce the result.

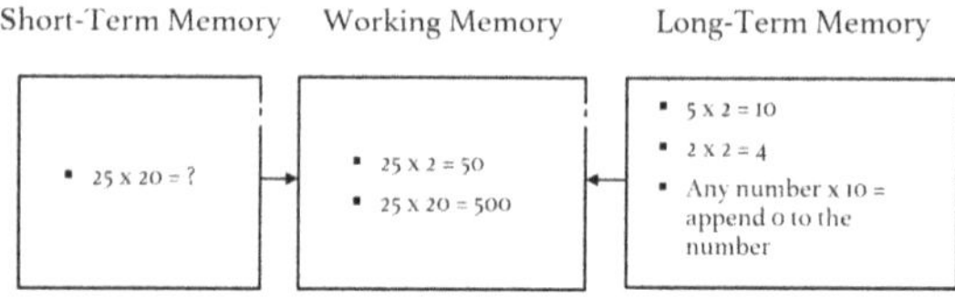

How Working Memory Works

Your working memory calculates 25 x 2 = 50. While holding onto this number, you retrieve from long-term memory that any number x 10 = append 0 to the number. You retrieve from short-term memory again that the question is 25 x 20 and work in your working memory to produce 500.

As your brainpower declines with age, your memory's ability to process, store, and remember information declines. You can prevent that by using your memory.

Memory Consolidation

Each day all the experience and stimuli you feed to your brain are stored into your long-term memory.[1] The process of transferring information from short-term memory to long-term memory is called consolidation. This process is delicate. Any interruption to the memory, even a minor disruption, can obliterate the memory before the consolidation occurs or even halt the consolidation. For example, you may abruptly forget what you went to the kitchen for as you walked into the kitchen.

Information in short-term memory is not transferred to long-term memory immediately. Some theories suggest that it takes about an hour or so after the initial learning for the consolidation to happen.[2]

Neuroscientists hypothesised that the consolidation process occurs mainly during REM (rapid eye movement) sleep. During the memory consolidation, the plasticity of your brain is effected, and any skill that you learn during the day gets mapped into your brain.

When you sleep, you go through four different stages of sleep.

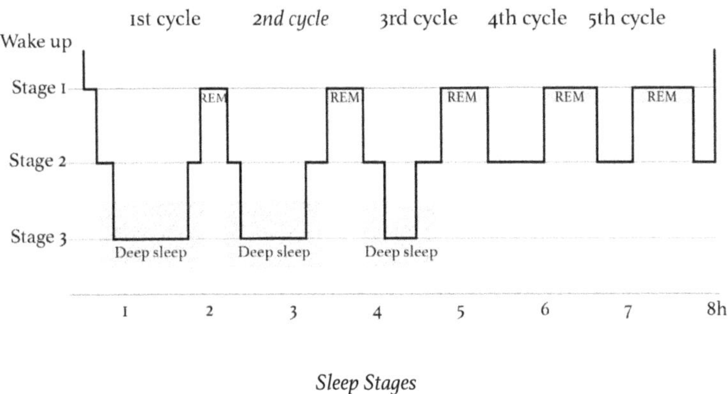

Sleep Stages

You dream at REM stage, which makes up about 25 percent of your sleep period. As you sleep longer, the duration of REM stage gets longer. This means, if you don't sleep long enough, you sacrifice REM sleep the most. If you want to maximize the amount of knowledge that can be stored in your long-term memory, you should get a long enough REM duration during your sleep.

Cramming last-minute study for a next-day examination and sleeping late are not a good idea. You would not remember most of what you have learned because you didn't get enough REM sleep to consolidate what you have learned into your long-term memory. Some proponents advocate sleeping less to increase productivity. But by cutting down your sleep, anything that you learn throughout the day is not fully stored into your long-term memory. That's a lot of learning hours gone to waste.

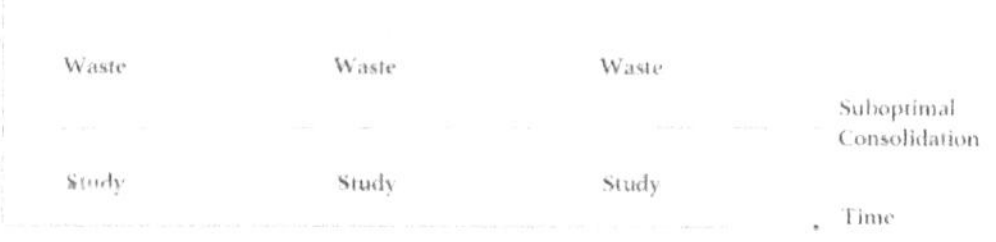

Infrequent and Crammed Learning with Less Sleep

It makes more sense to learn every day and store new knowledge daily with sufficient sleep, instead of cramming everything in a single day.

Frequent Learning with Optimal Sleep

SLEEP IS an important factor in neuroplasticity, and you should make an effort to make sure you have good quality sleep. I have detailed the full steps to get good quality sleep in another book, *Peak Human Clock*, if you haven't read that yet. When you are sleep-deprived, you shorten your overall sleep duration, including REM stage. Never try to shorten your sleep in the name of high productivity. Doing so only blunts your learning capacity.

Enhancing Learning

Learning is futile if you cannot remember what you have learned, which limits the knowledge application. Let's look at the methods to strengthen your learning and remember more.

Memory gradually fades with time unless it is recalled to be used. Even if you have forgotten about the memory, it is worth noting that the number of neuronal connections of that memory in your long-term memory is still higher than it was before you first learned it. That's why it is much easier to learn the same thing for the second time compared to when you learned it for the first time.

Not all memories fade at the same rate. Some decay easily, while others stick almost permanently. It goes without saying that you need high concentration to fortify and conceptualize your learning. Intense concentration also forges the path to neuroplasticity and reduces the chance of disrupting the memory consolidation process. Both traumatic experiences and euphoric moments evoke such a high concentration that makes them almost impossible to forget. Obviously, you don't have to experience these emotional states when you are trying to learn something. You should, however, aim to give your full concentration to your study materials. Intense attention makes learning stick better.

Some common mistakes most people make are:

1. Speed-reading

Don't fall prey to the idea that increasing your reading speed increases your learning speed. People have long hailed the technique of speed-reading to learn what you need to know quickly. But increasing your reading speed creates an overflow of information for your working memory to hold before transferring it to long-term memory. There is only so much that your working memory can process, and it will leave out most of the information. You end up only processing a little chunk of information without grasping the full context, even though you are under the illusion that you are processing all of it. Doing so sacrifices the most important part of learning: comprehension. Speed-reading equals less comprehension. Speed-reading is not speed-learning. Read your material mindfully. Pause to grasp each concept and reread as needed.

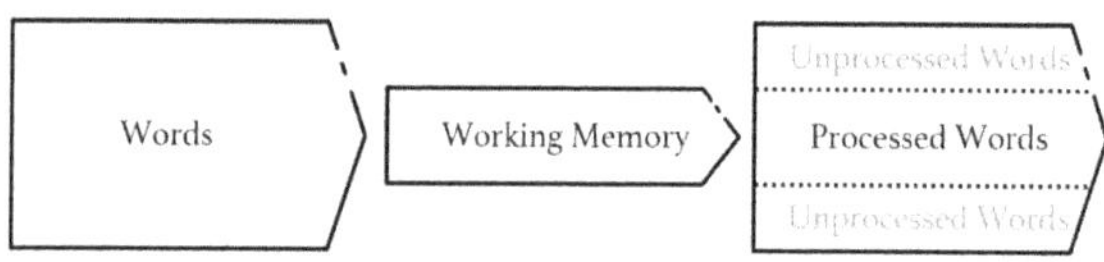

Working Memory Processing Speed-Read Information

2. Listening to music

Most people listen to music while studying. Indeed, it feels calming and motivating. Many students swear that they feel more focused and less stressed when listening to music while studying. However, this divides your attention between studying and listening to music. You are not giving your full attention to study alone. Research in 2018 showed that listening to music impairs reading comprehension.[3]

The tendency to use music on every occasion is formed by the indulgence of modern life. In almost everywhere you go, you get to listen to some music: the background music in a shopping mall, the uplifting music in a gym, and the music from your headphones when you walk outside. As you continue to constantly indulge your brain with distractions, your brain wants more distractions every time. It gets to the point that you feel you must listen to music before you start working.

You need to stop feeding this idea to your brain if you wish to have undivided attention for studying. It may feel unnatural and irritating when you first try to study without music, but you will notice the difference after two to four weeks of quitting it. Afterward, you will no longer crave music when you are working on something. You, in turn, feel distracted listening to it while working. You get to once again enjoy and immerse yourself in music when you listen to it deliberately.

Building more neuronal connections to the subject that you are learning solidifies the information and helps it persist longer. This can be achieved by helping your brain store information more effectively, as follows:

1. Connect new information with existing knowledge

Having existing related knowledge before learning new information makes learning much easier. Let's use a simple example below:

> New learning: Mars is a red planet with the tallest planetary mountain, called Mount Olympus.
> Existing knowledge: The mythological Roman god of war, Mars, lived on Mount Olympus.

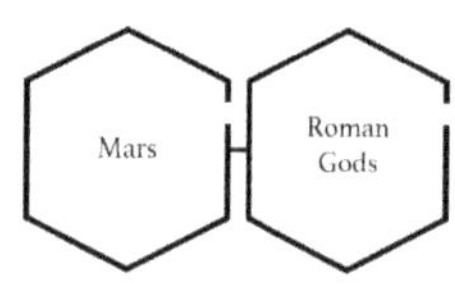

With your prior knowledge already well-established in memory, you can connect this new learning directly to your existing knowledge, and you now know that Mars is red because it symbolizes the spill of blood from the god of war. Its tallest mountain is named after the residence of the god. This helps you comprehend the subject much easier —even if no one taught you about this relationship. All of these are possible by connecting your new knowledge with an existing one.

If you don't have this existing knowledge and this is the first time that you are learning about the planet, you may have difficulty conceptualizing all the elements of the planet. Your limited-capacity working memory struggles more to absorb the new learning about Mars when compared to if you already knew the related previous knowledge. Maximizing learning requires that you use the limited capacity of your working memory as efficiently as possible to take in what you are learning, instead of working on the missing piece of information while learning at the same time. Amassing more knowledge for yourself allows your working memory to learn more things easily. Learn more to learn even more.

Most parents would protest if their children were allowed to use a calculator to solve mathematic problems on tests out of fear that it would blunt their calculation skills. However, using a calculator when solving mathematic problems reduces the resources of the working memory. Students can use more working memory to deepen their engagement with the mathematic problems without worrying about computational mistakes, and therefore, this increases their material comprehension. Research has shown that children who used calculators had higher test scores in problem-solving and showed higher aptitudes for mathematics compared to those who didn't use them.[4]

2. Learn other variations of the subject

Learning other variations of the same subject allows you to learn the subject easier because you can form broader connections and derive more knowledge out of it.

For example, if you are learning about praying mantises, you can learn the variety of things about it.

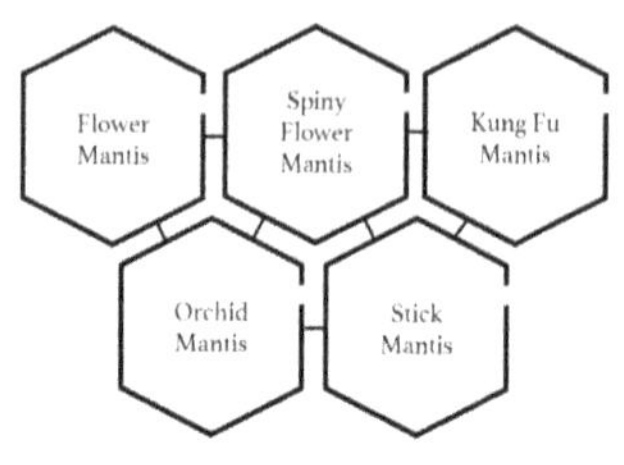

By learning different variations, you will feel slow initially because you are expending your time to learn all varieties. This gives you the perception that you are not learning fast. However, once you learn a variety of information on the subject, your level of understanding the unifying attributes increases. You also improve your ability to categorize and differentiate new types of praying mantises that you don't know yet, next time. This type of learning allows you to form more new connections to the subject after analyzing their similarities and differences, compared to those that narrow down the learning to a specific subject. In this example, you can form the following new connections:

- All mantises spread their forelegs to mount a defense.
- Mantises are not always green.
- All mantises have triangular heads with big eyes.

This method proves to work better for more durable learning, even though it takes longer. Learn slower now to learn faster later.

3. Brainstorm your own solutions

When you are presented with a problem, trying to solve the problem on your own before revealing the solution enables faster learning, even if your solution is incorrect. Attempting to solve the problem fires up your neurons to strengthen the possible connections to your existing knowledge. When you are given the correct answer later, you have paved the route in your brain to connect the answer to what you already know. Your brain will discard the memory of your incorrect answers and reconsolidate so it becomes easier for you to remember the correct answer next time.

For example, let's say you've been asked, "How do matadors enrage bulls?" When you brainstorm for possible answers, you would think through the logical explanation for each of them.

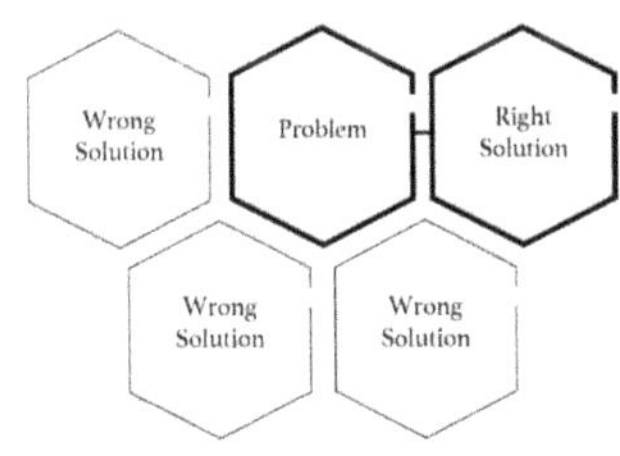

> "Maybe the red color of the cape? If so, then anyone wearing red would be in trouble."
> "Maybe the bull does not like the matador's attire? Hmm...how does a bull perceive human fashion?"

When an answer is given later that the bull is provoked by the actions of the matador, your brain updates the new information and removes the connection it has with other incorrect answers. The new information is further supported with more information from your brainstormed solutions.

> "Even though red cape is commonly used, other colors work, too."
> "The matador's attire has nothing to do with angry bulls."

4. Develop sensory associations

Associating a learning material with your experience or fictionalized stories enables enhanced learning because of the multi-sensory activation—sight, touch, hearing, taste, or smell —that fires multiple neurons together. Have you encountered a situation when you smelled a certain perfume, and you suddenly remembered a specific past event vividly that has long been forgotten? That smell is the context associated in your memory during the event. People learn better through experience because of this multi-sensory co-activation.

Not everyone has the chance to experience the subject they are learning. Fortunately, you can use the power of imagination to implant vivid stories in your brain. Learning by association creates more neural connections that makes remembering easier. The more you can associate your learning with your five senses, the more solid your learning is. Out of these sensory systems, visual information serves memory the best. So, use visualization as your main learning tool, while using the remaining sensory systems to support the memorization.

For example, if you find it hard to learn accounting terms, such as "accounts receivable," visualize an imaginary merchant who has promised to pay for your goods next month. The money would reach you within a month. See the story come to life. In your imagination, touch the goods you hand over to the merchant, hear him saying that he will make the payment next month, smell the indoor warehouse when the transaction takes place, taste the goods when he asks you to verify the authenticity of the product.

Note: "Accounts receivable" means all the sales a company has made but not collected the payment on yet.

5. Choose subjects that matter to you

When you learn a subject that matters to you, the knowledge sticks more firmly in your brain. This is because of your heightened curiosity, interest, and emotion. Strong emotion is one of the keys that induces neuroplasticity. If you have no interest in gardening, learning to garden is less personal to you and therefore less memorable to you.

It is important that you pick subjects of interest for your college or university study to maximize your learning potential. Sometimes you have no choice of what subjects to learn. Intentionally building interest in the subjects is helpful to improve your learning journey.

Maximizing Remembering

In 1880, a German psychologist named Hermann Ebbinghaus performed an experiment on how well the human brain can retain information. With no effort made to remember something, you will forget around 50 percent of what you learn within an hour, and 80 percent by the end of the month. Scientists replicated the same conclusion in 2015 successfully.[5]

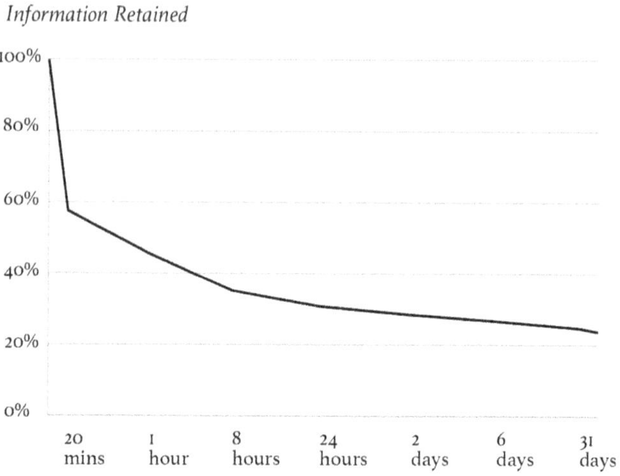

The Forgetting Curve

Back when I was in school, my teachers, tutors, and parents encouraged the practice of reciting learning materials to commit them into memory. Students were required to answer verbatim. Repeatedly reading the study material aloud seemed like a good way of learning and boosting my confidence because it gave the perception of remembering it immediately. Thirty minutes before an exam, I would see many of my classmates rereading the exam material religiously, and so did I. But during the exam, I would struggle to remember what I had read twenty minutes earlier, even though I was 100 percent certain that I had remembered it when I had read it. That was because I was relying on my short-term memory to memorize what I read. We have learned that short-term memory only lasts for about twenty seconds and can hold five to nine items. As I read subsequent chapters of the exam material, even though I reread them aloud to myself, I had replaced the previous material with the new one in my memory—forgetting the older material.

To remember any information for a long time, you need to practice recalling, and not just reciting what you have read. Your brain reconstructs the information that you have stored, which means the recalled information can be altered or partially forgotten. As you recall or use the information from your long-term memory often, you readjust the neuronal connections to the information and make the memory more vivid. This explains why you remember your phone number easily but don't remember the formula of the Pythagorean theorem you learned in high school. You recall your phone number many more times than you do the Pythagorean theorem. The phone number is stored solidly in your long-term memory.

Recalling information involves the following processes:

1. Recalling the memory from long-term memory to short-term memory.

2. Updating the memory, erasing some invalid memory, or keeping the same memory.

3. Reconsolidating the memory from short-term memory back to long-term memory.

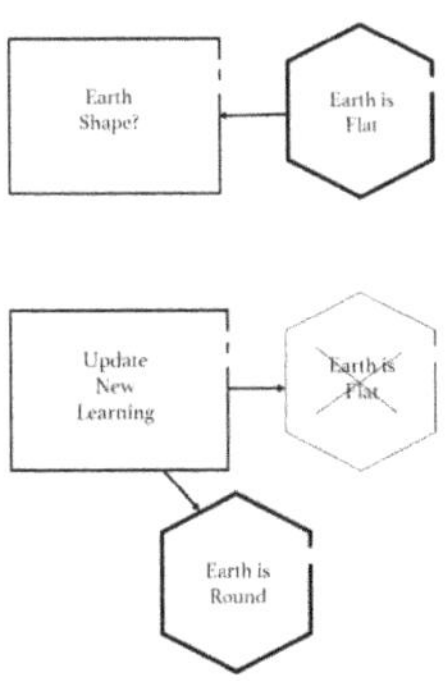

. . .

NOTICE THAT RECONSOLIDATION happens every time you recall something from your long-term memory. The information is brought into short-term memory again before reconsolidating it back to long-term memory. You overwrite your old memory with the new memory. The next time you recall the information, you will retrieve the new memory.

While recalling, you also risk updating the memory with the wrong information and reconsolidating it incorrectly back into long-term memory. Psychologists conducted an experiment in 1974 to verify if a single word could alter a recalled memory.[6] They gathered forty-five students to show them a car accident video. After watching the video, each student was asked one of five questions:

- About how fast were the cars going when they ***smashed*** each other?
- About how fast were the cars going when they ***collided with*** each other?
- About how fast were the cars going when they ***bumped*** each other?
- About how fast were the cars going when they ***hit*** each other?
- About how fast were the cars going when they ***contacted*** each other?

The experiment showed that students remembered the accident to be faster when asked the question containing the verb "***smashed***," compared to others. Their original memory has been altered during the recalling process because of the questions asked. Therefore, it is important that inspectors must not allow witnesses to talk to each other before an interrogation happens. Each conversation bears risk of altering the true memory.

The experience of déjà vu ensues when you cannot completely recall the event from your long-term memory. Those fragmented memories give you the feeling of familiarity that makes you believe that you have reexperienced the same event in the past.

The more effort needed to recall the information, the stronger the neuronal connections, and the easier it is to recall next time. The less effort needed to recall the information, the weaker the neuronal connections, and the more difficult it is to recall next time.

To solidify the memory of the information that you are learning, make your recalling effort more challenging by deliberately letting the memory fade. Let the memory fade for some time before attempting to recall the information. For example, after learning a specific piece of information, you can try to recall the information a few days later. When you successfully recall the information, you strengthen the memory pathway. The frequency must not be too frequent that you need less effort to recall and not too infrequent that makes recalling impossible. Recalling must be successful to strengthen the neuronal connections.

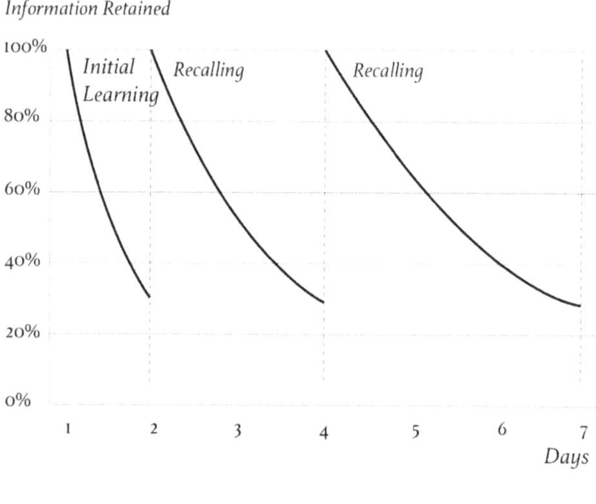

Spaced-Out Recalling

When you study for an examination, recalling the information after waiting some time also allows you to judge yourself accurately on whether you truly remember the material and gives you a chance to relearn if you have forgotten about it.

Memorizing Techniques

Before we begin, you can forget about the myth that people with photographic memories can magically memorize large amounts of information without any effort. Even memory masters deploy some memorization techniques to memorize large items. It is just not biologically possible for the human working memory to hold an extensive amount of information.

Let's explore some techniques to memorize anything with ease. Often, things that you need to memorize have no context for you to comprehend, and you simply need to memorize them:

for example, a capital city, a Latin name, or a word in a foreign language made up of only symbols. You have no way to link these words to any of your existing knowledge, nor can you brainstorm any solution before learning them. Thus, you are left with using just the ***association*** technique. And, because you can only use one technique, you want to really maximize its effect. Summon all your five sensory functions to strengthen your memory associations. Make the associated story as silly as possible to evoke emotion and fire multiple neurons.

Memorizing words

Let's try to learn the French word for ***egg***: ***"oeuf."*** The word sounds like "earth." Make a story of an earth and an egg.

- **Sight:** Visualize that the ***earth*** was first formed together with a large ***egg***.
- **Touch:** You touched the slimy egg and felt the slime.
- **Smell:** Unexpectedly, it smelled fragrant.
- **Taste:** You licked the eggshell, and it tasted salty. *Did someone preserve the egg with brine solution?* you wondered.
- **Hearing:** Suddenly you heard an earthquake, and the egg cracked. To your surprise, Adam came out of the egg.

Now, let's try doing this with the scientific name for ***mosquito***: "***Culicidae***." The word sounds like "kill it seed die." This could be the story.

- **Sight**: Visualize two female mosquitoes who were hunting for food. Unable to find any human blood to drink, they saw a seed on an uncovered trash can.
- **Hearing**: You heard them discussing whether there was any blood in the seed to suck. One mosquito refused the other's suggestion to eat it, saying, "if you ***kill it, seed die***."
- **Taste**: The other mosquito went on to suck the blood out of the seed. You tried to taste the spilled blood, and it tasted metallic.
- **Smell**: It smelled metallic, too, like human blood.
- **Touch**: You touched the seed that has died. The thick blood felt sticky.

Apply the same principles when you learn foreign words that are made of symbols, such as Chinese, Japanese, or Korean.

Let's learn a Chinese word: ***sugar***. This is how I see the word in my brain.

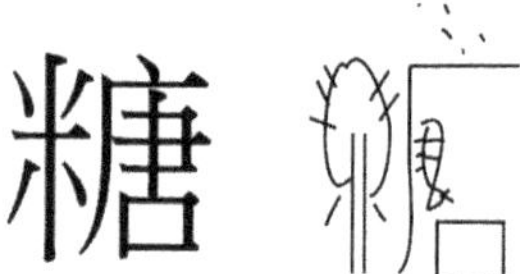

My Imaginary Image of a Chinese Character, Sugar

Here's a story you could use: An ant was walking down a house wall to pick up a cube of ***sugar*** while it was raining outside. There was a pine tree beside the house.

Also, these languages include many common strokes that are used in a variety of words. You can create a story or visualize a character for each of those common strokes as you encounter them. For example, the stroke represented by the tree image inside the Chinese word of sugar is used in many other Chinese words. Whenever you learn a new Chinese word that contains a common stroke, integrate the word's individual story with the whole story by using the same images. This saves you time on figuring out what image to use. During the recalling process, you also ascertain from your memory that it is a common stroke you have used before. Watch out for common strokes that look similar but not the same. They confer different meanings. In such a case, create a different image for it so as not to confuse your memory.

I learned to write one to three new Chinese words daily. I wrote the same character about twenty times. However, if I gave myself a test, I would not remember how to write what I had learned a week ago, and sometimes not even the ones I had learned a day before. I then changed the way I learned by practicing ***recalling***. I learned two words every day and gave myself a day to let myself almost forget about the words before I tested myself to recall all the previous words I had learned. Retesting after twenty-four hours gave ample time for my memory to forget and made recalling more effortful. It was also not too long that it would make me completely forget what I had learned. I was startled by the high number of words I could then recall daily. It was an enormous improvement compared to how I did previously.

What was more surprising was, in the middle of my learning, I also decided to apply an ***association*** technique. The outcome was even better. I could remember most of the words I had learned, and sometimes all of them. Note that I specifically picked moderate to high complexity words to learn in this experiment. I would skip the easy ones so I didn't distort the outcome. Here's the data.

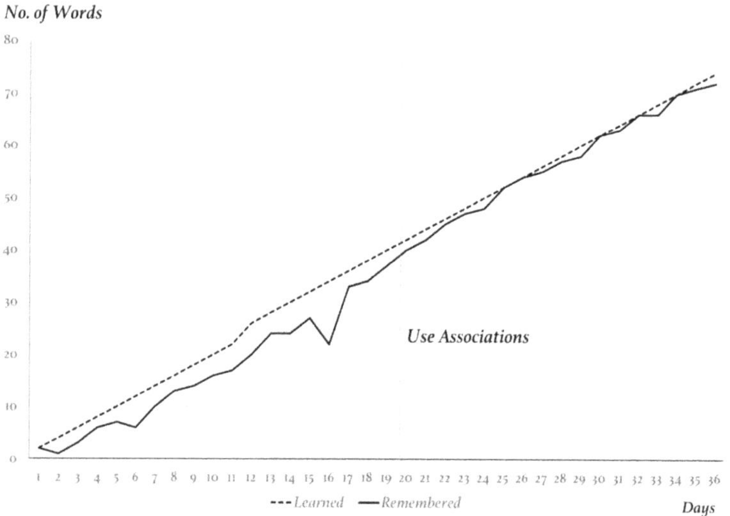

Number of Words Learned and Forgotten

On average, I spent about eleven minutes to test myself and seven minutes to learn two new words, which totaled up to about seventeen minutes learning time daily. That's a sprinkling of time anyone can invest to learn a new language. As you begin to remember most of the words, the testing time reduces even though you need to write the entire vocabulary you have learned. Once you have grown a long list, say a hundred words, you can space out the testing and do half of them each on every alternate day.

With this method, you can learn sixty words well every month. There is no reason that you can't learn any new language if you can just carve out less than thirty minutes out of your schedule every day. If you exercised this technique for a year, you'd learn 730 new words. All you need is the learning material, some creativity, and some willpower. No tuition fee needed. By the way, I wrote a book on maximizing willpower, *Peak Self-Control*, in case you haven't read that yet.

Memorizing Numbers

The maximum amount of pieces of information that you can hold in your memory is five to nine items. In particular, no one can memorize large amounts of numbers with just their short-term memory. Numbers aren't visual, so if you want to maximize the power of memorizing them, you need to turn each one into a visual image.

You need to encode the number into an image, try to remember the image, and store it into your memory. When you need to recall the number, you need to remember the image and decode the image back into a number. Let's try this with short numbers.

Method for short numbers:

A simple method is to visualize each number as an image it resembles. For example, number **2** could look like a snake, and number **6** could look like a rope.

- When you want to memorize number **26**, you visualize a snake (**2**) wrapping around a rope (**6**).
- When you want to memorize number **62**, you visualize a rope (**6**) tying up a snake (**2**).

This method presents limited applicability on the amount of numbers you can memorize because:

1. You are constrained to just ten images for each number from zero to nine, and
2. You need to memorize two images for two digits, which uses more resources in your working memory and isn't economical for large numbers.

If you have problems memorizing short numbers and need a quick solution, you can adopt this method. But if you want to memorize large numbers, check out the next method.

Method for long numbers:

THIS METHOD IS CALLED the ***major system*** and requires some time to practice before you can use it correctly. Once you master this, you can memorize any number, short or long. I learned this method from the international memory grandmaster, Kevin Horsley. This method requires you to convert chunks of numbers into images in your brain to remember large numbers easily.

It starts the same as the previous method, but this time we are going to need an additional step to convert the number to a letter of the alphabet first before visualizing an image for it.

It sounds complicated, but with ample practice, this will be easy for you. Practice until your brain can see a letter easily just by calling out the matching number. As an analogy, when you master this, your brain will be able to convert numbers to images as fast as it probably already does for the following numbers:

- 101: Beginner lesson
- 007: James Bond
- 911: Police

Practicing this will take a lot of time; however, the benefits quickly pay off. If you practice this every day, you may be able to master it in two to three months. You will come to embrace the beauty of this technique. You can use this to memorize everything that is represented in numbers, such as date of events, postal codes, phone numbers, or bank account numbers. The amount of numbers that you can remember is very large.

To make this method effective, you need to first invest your time to get accustomed to the number-letter conversion. Let's begin.

Step 1:

Familiarize yourself with the following number-letter mappings and the tricks to remember them:

- 0 = S, Z, soft C — The sound of these resembles the faint hissing sound of a deflating tire.
- 1 = T, D — Both downstrokes resemble number one, and "T" and "D" sound similar.
- 2 = N — Rotate "N" 90 degrees clockwise, and it forms number two.
- 3 = M — Rotate lowercase "m" 90 degrees clockwise, and it forms number three.
- 4 = R — "R" almost looks like a mirror of number four.
- 5 = L — "L" is the Roman numeral for fifty.
- 6 = J, SH, soft CH, soft G — "J" and lowercase "g" almost look like flipped variations of number six. "SH" and "CH" sound similar to "J" and "G."
- 7 = K, hard C — "K" looks similar to number seven. "C" sounds almost like "K."
- 8 = F, V — Cursive lowercase "f" looks like number eight. "V" sounds almost like "F."
- 9 = B, P — "P" and lowercase "b" look like number nine when flipped different ways.

THIS LIST MAY PRESENT a challenge for those whose mother tongue is not English, including myself, because it is difficult to discern the letters that sound soft and hard. I have revised this list to be as follows for my usage. You can use any list that works best for you.

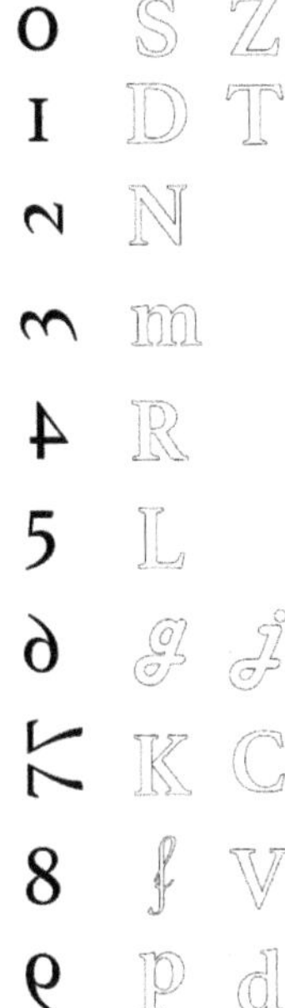

Amended Major System List

The remaining alphabets have no mapping, and you can use them to form words in the next step.

Go through this list many times until it becomes second nature to you. This list serves as the foundation, and you need to make sure this list sticks in your long-term memory. It is not efficient for you to use your working memory to hold onto this list when you are trying to memorize your numbers. If you still need a long time to recall these, you are not ready to proceed to the next step.

Step 2:

PRACTICE CONVERTING two-digit numbers to letters and then to words. The word that you form must be a ***noun*** instead of ***an adjective***, ***a verb***, or ***a preposition***. This is because nouns are easier to visualize than other parts of speech. You don't have to follow my list below. Using your own words will be more memorable and familiar for you.

- 01 - **SeeD**
- 02 - **ZoNe**
- 03 - **SuMo**
- 04 - **ZoRo**
- 09 - **SaiD** (my name)

Proceed to the next step after you reach number 99.

Step 3:

BY NOW, mapping numbers to letters should be easy for you. The challenge is using your creativity to turn the letters into words. Practice converting three-digit numbers to letters and then to words. Again, use your own words that you are already familiar with. It's tempting to use more than one word for three-digit numbers. However as much as possible, try to come up with just one word to reduce the number of words that you need to memorize. You will see how this can help you when you are at step 4.

- 001 - **SieSTa**

- 164 - TiGeR
- 170 - TaCoS
- 340 - MaRS
- 907 - BaZooKa
- 911 - PoTaTo

You don't have to practice from 000 to 999. If you can convert a random word easily into a three-digit random number, you are ready to proceed to the next step. You can save your list, too, so that whenever you need to memorize a number, you can refer to your list instead of coming up with another list again. Challenge yourself to map four-digit numbers, such as "2015 - **NeSTLe.**" If you can't think of a word for large digit numbers, split them into chunks of two-digit numbers or three-digit numbers.

Step 4:

Now let the fun begin. Say you want to memorize this piece of information:

> "Singapore declared independence in 1965."

FORM A WORD WITH **1965**, for example **ToP GoaL**. Create a story to associate "top goal" with "Singapore's independence."

Here's my version:

- **Sight:** Visualize a vivid image of the iconic merlion competing in a soccer match to win independence.

Having no legs, the merlion must squirt water to dribble the ball.

- **Touch:** The squirt was wrongly fired at your face. It hurt, and the water felt icy cold. It seemed that the merlion was storing the water in a freezing stomach.
- **Smell:** The water smelled like sparkling water. Perhaps its stomach has a water carbonating processor.
- **Taste:** You tasted the water, and it indeed tasted like sparkling water.
- **Hearing:** While you were still being sprayed with the water, you heard a national anthem being played. The merlion has won independence. You heard the announcer say it scored the top goal of the year with its unique dribbling style.

Note: A merlion is a mythical creature with a lion's head and the body of fish. It is the symbol of Singapore.

Close your eyes and replay this scene in your head. Take your time to interact with the scene in your mind. When you are done, the "top goal" and "Singapore's independence" association should stick in your memory.

Earlier I mentioned that you need to store the number-letter mapping into your long-term memory. The below illustration depicts how your brain operates when you attempt to memorize numbers without having the number-letter mapping available into your long-term memory. Notice that you need to force your working memory to hold onto too much information at once, which reduces its capacity to remember the real numbers.

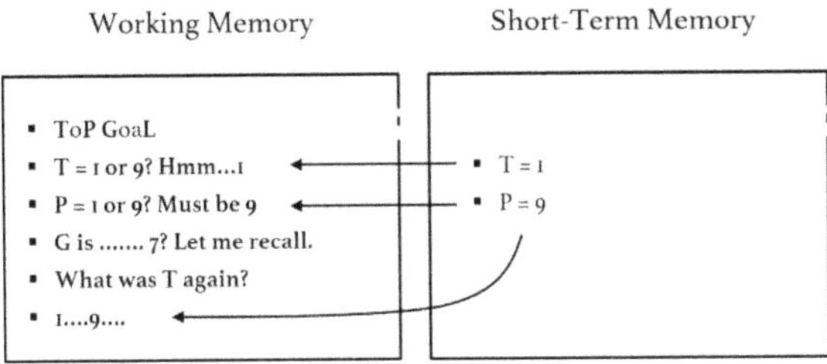

Reliance on Short-Term Memory

And the below illustration shows how your brain operates when you have the mapping ready in your long-term memory:

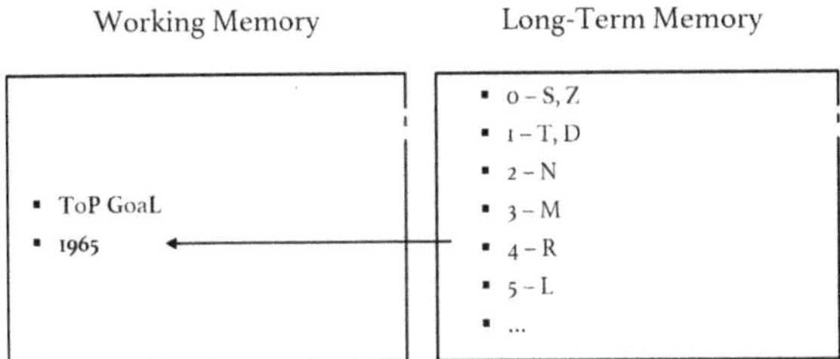

Reliance on Long-Term Memory

By relying on long-term memory, you only need to use your working memory to construct the image. Certainly, this is a more efficient approach, and you have more space to remember more numbers.

Memorizing Sequences

There are times when memorizing individual words and numbers is not enough, and you need to memorize them in a fixed sequence. We will learn a new technique to memorize a sequence and repurpose what we have learned earlier about memorizing words and numbers.

Method for a short list:

This method uses a ***rhyming peg.*** You use words that rhyme with a given number. For example:

- 1 - Bun
- 2 - Shoe
- 3 - Tree
- 4 - Boar
- 5 - Knife
- 6 - Sticks
- 7 - Heaven
- 8 - Gate
- 9 - Vine
- 10 - Pen

Let's say that you want to memorize *Maslow's Hierarchy of Needs*. Peg each item to this list and create a story for them sequentially:

1. Physiological needs (food, water, warmth, rest): A street full of ***buns*** to feed the ***hunger***.
2. Safety needs (security, safety): You need to wear a pair of ***shoes*** to ***protect*** your feet in case you step on a porcupine.
3. Love needs (relationships, friends): A couple ***kissing*** under a ***tree***.

4. Esteem needs (prestige): King Robert Baratheon lost his ***prestige*** after being killed by a ***boar***.
5. Self-actualization (achieving one's full potential): Salt Bae realized his ***full potential*** with his amazing ***knife*** skill.

REMEMBER to engage all your five senses to reenact each story.

Method for a long list:

THIS TECHNIQUE USES A *MEMORY PALACE*. It is an imaginary or real location in your mind that you can use to store mnemonic pegs.

Step 1:

RETRIEVE a set of information in your long-term memory that has a long sequence. You likely already have one in your mind. Maybe a sequence of your house interior layout from your front door to the last room, or the journey from your house to the office. Make sure you have the fixed sequential order of your *memory palace*. For simplicity, the words below could be a sequence of a house layout:

1. **Entrance:** doorbell, front gate, main entrance
2. **Living Room**: coffee table, TV, TV console
3. **Dining Room**: dining room entrance, dining table, dining chair 1, dining chair 2
4. **Kitchen**: kitchen entrance, refrigerator

5. **Bedroom:** bedroom door, bedroom entrance, study table, bed, bedside table

The longer the list, the better suited it is for a larger sequence. Remember that you must get this from your existing long-term memory. Creating one during the process of memorization is not efficient for your working memory.

If you don't have one, form one with at least twenty sequences and attempt to remember it. Make sure that you can call it out easily before proceeding with the next step.

Step 2:

LET'S try to remember a hundred digits of the sequence of phi decimals.

3.1415926535897932384626433832795028
84197169399375105820974944592307816
4062862089986280348253421170679

Split these numbers into chunks of numbers using the *major system* we learned earlier, and form word(s) for each of them. The more digits you can convert into a single word, the better because you shorten the number of items to memorize. My version goes like this:

141592|653|589|7932|384|6264|338|
327950|2884|1971|693|99|3751|058|
2097|4944|592307|816|40|628|620|

89|98|628|034|8253|421|170|679

TuRTLe BeaN|GoLeM|LiFeBuoy|ChaPMaN|May-FaiR|GiNGeR|hoMe MoVie|MuNiCiPaL houSe|NaVy oF iRaq|DuBai CiTy|GP3|PaPaya|hoMe ChiLD|SaLiVa|NoSePieCe|waR PRayeR|LiByaN MuSiC|FooTaGe|hoRSe|GeNeVa|GaNeSha|ViP|Bee-hiVe|GeNeVa|SaMuRai|FiNaL exaM|hoRNeT|wiTCheS|JuKeBox

Step 3:

Now we have twenty-nine items to map into our *memory palace*. We will use the sample house layout to map these. Here is my storyline:

- Doorbell — Turtle bean: As I pressed the square doorbell to enter a house, a handful of black **turtle beans** fell from the doorbell. It seemed that someone placed the turtle beans on the doorbell.
- Front gate — Golem: A **golem** opened the front gate to let me in.
- Main entrance — Lifebuoy, chapman, Mayfair: I walked in and stepped on a ***Lifebuoy*** soap on the floor and fell on the ground. A **chapman** then lifted me up and offered to sell me a ticket to the **Mayfair** at a discounted rate. I rejected the offer and walked into the living room.
- Coffee table — Ginger: I smelled ginger scent. The

ginger on the coffee table must have been placed there to make the living room smell good.

- TV — Home movie: In front of the sofa, there is a **home movie** playing on a TV.
- TV console — Municipal House: On the TV console, there was a Lego building of a **Municipal House.**
- Dining room entrance — Navy of Iraq, Dubai city, GP3: A man then led me to the dining room. He was in the **navy of Iraq.** He asked me to join him in **Dubai city** to watch the **GP3** (Grand Prix 3) race.
- Dining table — Papaya: I saw a piece of **papaya** on the dining table.
- Dining chair 1 — Home child, saliva: There was a **home child** looking longingly at the papaya. I could see his **saliva** dripping on the chair.
- Dining chair 2 — Nosepiece, war prayer: Next to the child, I saw a woman wearing a **nosepiece** reading the ***War Prayer*** poem to the child.
- Kitchen entrance — Libyan music, footage, horse: I walked to the kitchen, and a man showed me a video. The video began with **Libyan music** playing in the background, followed by **footage** of a **horse.**
- Refrigerator — Geneva, Ganesha: I walked to the refrigerator and saw a bottle of wine from **Geneva** and a statue of **Ganesha.** It seemed that someone just returned from Geneva.
- Bedroom door — VIP: I then walked to the bedroom; there was a label "**VIP**" on the door. I wondered who was inside.
- Bedroom entrance — Beehive: As I stepped into the

room, I accidentally hit a hanging **beehive** and was soon swarmed by bees.

- Study table — Geneva, samurai, final exam: I saved myself from the bees' attack and walked into the room. There was a man from **Geneva** writing on the table and a **samurai** pointing his katana at that man. I asked the samurai what was going on, and he told me that the man was preparing for his **final exam.**
- Bed — Hornet, witches: I then walked to the bed and was stung by a **hornet.** The hornet may have nested in the same beehive I saw earlier. On the bed, two **witches** lay sleeping.
- Bedside table — Jukebox: At the bedside table, there was a **jukebox** playing. Apparently, the witches enjoyed playing a jukebox melody to fall asleep.

We have just used twenty-nine items to map in a memory palace a hundred-digit number. Remember to use your five sensory systems to experience this list. Run through this a few times, and you should be able to memorize this.

THE APPLICABILITY of these techniques is universal, and you can use them for any situation that requires memorizing. Try out for yourself with anything that you want to memorize. The only limit is your own imagination. You can set up your own memorization techniques, too, as long as you can peg the material of your learning into something that you can remember. You will realize that you too can memorize complicated matters. At the same time, practicing memorization also increases your neurogenesis rate.

It can be intimidating to learn these techniques. Consider it as the initial investment of your time to allow you to memorize anything else more easily later.

IN THE NEXT CHAPTER, we will look into one of the major hindrances that taxes your brain development: anxiety. We also will cover how to fix the root of the problem.

4

REWIRE AN ANXIOUS BRAIN

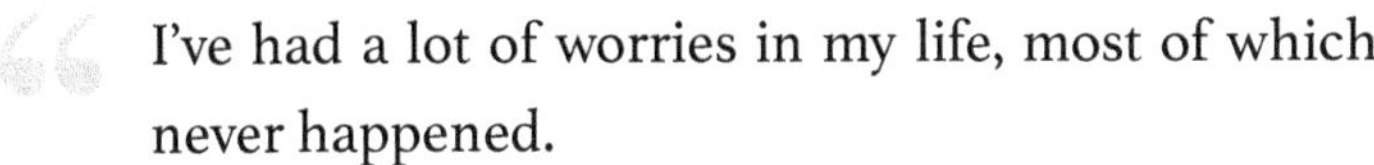

> I've had a lot of worries in my life, most of which never happened.
>
> — Mark Twain

Anxiety is a stressful experience that reduces neurogenesis. Anxiety and depression cost the global economy about $1 trillion in lost productivity.[1] It is saddening that many people do not get to *live* because of how paralyzing this mental problem is and how it preoccupies them in their daily lives. The time that could be spent learning and progressing is lost to worry. People sometimes cope with the problem by drinking alcohol or binge eating, further reducing their neurogenesis.

With anxiety plaguing our lives, our journey to hone our brainpower is hampered by the malaise and negative thoughts that reshape our brains to be worriers. We will figure out how anxiety starts in our brain and how to heal it from the inside out. To fix anxiety, it is important that you know the science behind it. Continuing to take anti-anxiety medication for the rest of your life will never cure it.

Please note that this book will only address the mild anxiety problems most of us experience. I am not qualified to treat severe forms of it, such as post-traumatic stress disorder, reactive attachment disorder, panic disorder, and other psychiatric disorders.

MOST OF US experience at least a mild form of anxiety. It all starts with chronic worrying that progresses to anxiety, which sometimes advances to depression. Blessed are those who have no anxiety.

Jill, an accountant, has been battling with anxiety since she started working. Her job is hectic. She often works late. From time to time, her boss texts her after office hours and demands that Jill complete a report for him within an hour. Being a person who does not want to disappoint others, she drops everything that she was doing and starts working on the report quickly. Her adrenaline rises while she works on the report to meet the unreasonable deadline. There have been a few times that she has produced slovenly work and her boss retorted with insulting words.

Her heart rate elevates every time the text message notification from her phone sounds; she worries that it may be her overbearing boss. She feels the same when the similar ringtone plays from her husband's phone.

She stops fully enjoying her evenings with her kids after work, and she has developed a tendency to constantly check her phone in case she misses her boss's texts.

When she lies in bed at night, she often thinks of different "what-ifs." What if she made a mistake in the report she just sent to her boss? What if her boss tried to contact her but she missed his text? What if her boss disliked her work? Self-doubt creeps in, and she replays in her head variations on how her boss may give her scathing remarks the next day.

How Anxiety Is Triggered

Let's look into the parts of the brain that play important roles in enacting this anxious cycle. There are three key parts of our brain involved, including:

1. **Prefrontal cortex.** This part allows you to do higher-level thinking and to reason, learn, plan, and anticipate results. You use this part of the brain to discern genuine threats from false threats.
2. **Limbic system.** This part includes your emotions and experiences. It has a small part called the ***amygdala*** that detects potential threats based on what you have experienced throughout your life to keep you safe. Another part of it is called the ***thalamus***, which relays messages from sensory organs to your brain.
3. **Reptilian brain.** This part ensures your survival by

regulating your heart rate, giving you the feeling of hunger, increasing your adrenaline to ***fight*** when you can overcome a threat, ***flee*** when you can't overcome a threat, or ***freeze*** to conserve your energy when you face an inescapable threat.

The fight/flight/freeze response can be activated in three ways:

1. Through the amygdala system

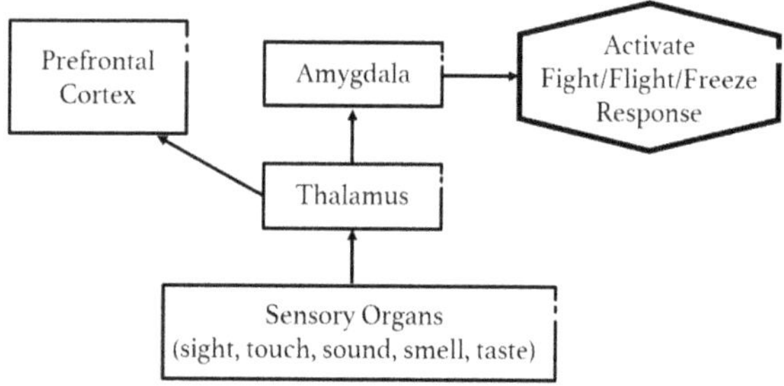

An Anxiety Response Triggered by the Amygdala System

Your sensory experiences are received by the thalamus, which relays the information to both your prefrontal cortex for higher-level processing and your amygdala to determine whether whatever you're experiencing is a threat. The amygdala only has one goal: to save your life. Its reaction is so fast that within less than a tenth of a second it can mobilize your bodily responses: increasing your heart rate, surging adrenaline through your veins, increasing your blood pressure, and heightening your senses to prepare you for battle. It has no time to waste consulting your prefrontal cortex of possible imminent danger. If it needs to consult your prefrontal cortex for every possible threat, you would not hear stories of a father instinctually swinging his arms to catch his infant who was falling off a sofa or of a driver's incredible split-second reaction to swerve and escape a road accident.

The amygdala continuously monitors your experiences and records potential threats. When you first touched a boiling kettle, your amygdala registered that and prevented you from repeating it next time. Its memory lasts forever. Whenever your amygdala recognizes a similar burning sensation on your skin, it will trigger the fight/flight/freeze response.

In Jill's case, as soon as the incoming text notification sounds, her amygdala has already surged her adrenaline and increased her nervousness before she even has a chance to think clearly that the incoming text could be from others. When she becomes aware of it, she is already overwhelmed by her increased heart rate and blood pressure.

You have no control over the rapid reactions that your amygdala triggers. When the fight/flight/freeze response is activated, your prefrontal cortex capacity is hampered. Survival comes first. You won't be able to think carefully. It is easy for anyone to tell her to calm down, forget about her boss, and start living again. Being a smart professional, she certainly knows that worrying about her work makes her feel worse. But she simply can't stop thinking about it. Her amygdala has already registered the worrisome experience. This is a biological problem and not a logical problem. That's why you can't solve it with logical advice or just tell her to forget about the work that she's turned in.

Sometimes you may not even remember or be aware of when your amygdala has registered a certain experience as a threat. You may encounter a situation where your heart pounds hard for no apparent reason, or suddenly your anxiety rushes out of nowhere, or you feel uncomfortably fearful in a certain place. All of these are your amygdala in action.

2. Through the prefrontal cortex system

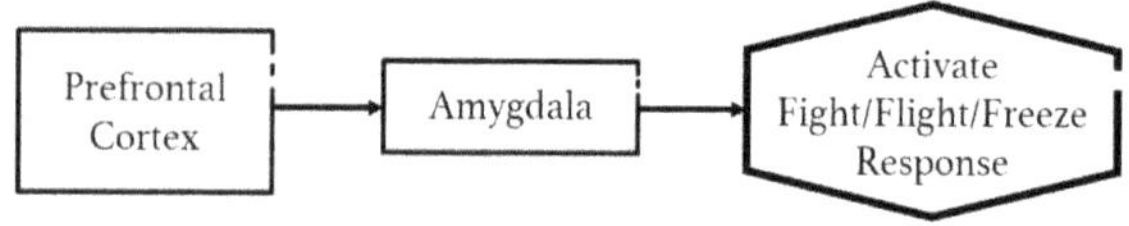

An Anxiety Response Triggered by the Prefrontal Cortex System

Your prefrontal cortex has an impressive capability to create and manipulate many images of thoughts. It can use imagination to create an experience at a subconscious level that resembles reality very closely. Imagining an experience in your brain activates the same brain response as if the experience is real.[2] When your prefrontal cortex generates anxious thoughts, the thoughts are sent to your amygdala, which then activates the anxiety response.

Sadly, an uncontrolled prefrontal cortex is a recipe for enhancing your anxiety. Often, worriers use their prefrontal cortex to imagine catastrophic scenarios that may never happen. In Jill's case, her prefrontal cortex thinks through different possibilities of events and anticipates the potential consequences of her work. As her prefrontal cortex creatively generates worrisome scenarios, it activates the amygdala to sound her fight-or-flight alarm system. She becomes nervous.

Her condition will only exacerbate as time passes. Every time the incoming text ringtone plays, her anxiety response is triggered and her brain's plasticity reshapes to reinforce that she must get ready to fight whenever she hears that ringtone. Every time she ruminates in her bed, her brain's plasticity reshapes to reinforce that she must ruminate before sleeping. As her brain reshapes, her anxiety will only increase.

If you have anxiety, the longer you leave it untreated, the harder it is to fix, for your brain has already taken a new shape. As for Jill, after years of reshaping her brain, her brain has structurally changed to associate anxiety with her phone's ringtone and lying in bed.

3. Through both the amygdala and prefrontal cortex systems

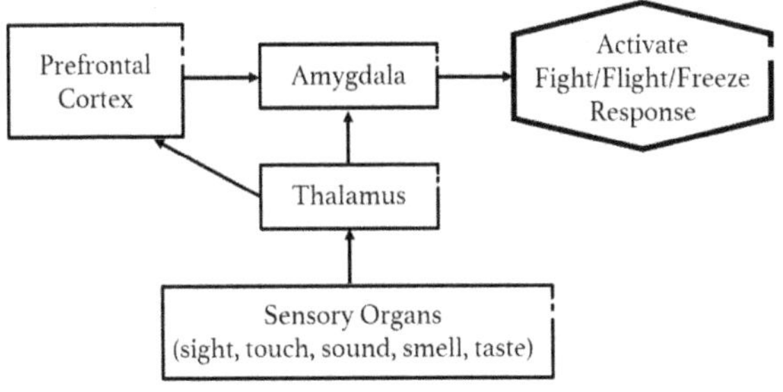

An Anxiety Response Triggered by Both the Prefrontal Cortex and Amygdala Systems

The reaction that goes through the prefrontal cortex pathway is slower compared to that that goes through the amygdala because your prefrontal cortex needs to transmit the information to the amygdala first before the amygdala can activate the anxiety response. But both the amygdala and prefrontal cortex could trigger your anxiety at the same time. While your amygdala receives a sense of threat and sounds the alarm, your prefrontal cortex imagines the worst-case scenario. This chain of events creates a cascading effect to heighten your anxiety response and prolong it.

Forget Your Worries

You may apply a variety of relaxation techniques to ease your anxious mind, but allow me to present you just three things that will fix the root of the problem. Given how anxiety can be triggered, the only solution is to train your brain to reshape it to a non-anxious brain. This is challenging to do but worth the effort.

1. Stop ruminating

We have learned that plasticity gets stronger as you repeat the same actions. Ruminating is a powerful avenue to worsen the anxiety. The more your brain ruminates, the better it ruminates. To people with anxiety, ruminating is a way to feel that they are in control of a situation. Had they not thought through different scenarios, they wouldn't feel ready to face the anticipated problems. Often, they don't realize that dwelling on the issue only helps their brains be more anxious. As you continue to dwell on the same self-defeating thoughts every day, your brain changes and craves doing that routinely. This results in a vicious cycle that further exacerbates your anxiety.

The catalyst for ruminating is often boredom. It is easy to fix this in the daytime by keeping yourself occupied: exercising, playing, working on a creative project, etc. But it is hard to stop ruminating while lying in bed. There is no simple way to interrupt your mind when you can't move around. The voice in your head can creep in to rehearse your worries when you have nothing to distract it. Trying to push the voice away will only cause it to return soon afterward. Your mind does not like unfinished business. Instead, accept your own voice and sincerely give it a conclusive answer to stop the loop. The conversation in your mind could go like this:

> "So, what you really want to tell me is that I may be doing careless work that may make my boss unhappy? I will improve myself next time."
> "Did the reply you sent to your boss offend him?"
> "I'm not sure, but I did not send it with the intent to offend."
> "He may send you another task and demand it done ASAP."
> "I can't help if he does that, but I will just see it tomorrow when I get to work. Let's sleep now. Thank you for your concern for me."

If you anticipate that you will ruminate at night, before going to bed, write on a piece of paper what your inner voice will speak, and write your answer, too. Make sure you write everything that bothers you—don't leave anything out. Fold the paper and store it somewhere; you may not go back to reread it, anyway. The thought that you have secured what you need to do helps to stop rumination.

As you begin to ruminate only rarely, you weaken the anxiety trigger that originates from your prefrontal cortex. It will take some time for your brain to take a new shape, but over time, you will solve half of the problem this way.

2. Update the amygdala's memory

After years of living in anxiety, your brain has already strengthened the connections that lead to anxiety. Your amygdala has stored the memories of every anxious experience. All your anxiety triggers must have been registered by your amygdala at some point in time. If you can find out the specific experience that first caused your anxiety, you can dissociate it in your memory.

If you were derided by your critical teacher or jeered at by your friends when you were giving a speech at school, you may be fearful to speak in front of an audience now. Your amygdala registered this as: ***giving a speech = threat to get belittled.***

For Jill, perhaps she received her boss' nasty tirade. Her embarrassment and high emotional state fired multiple neurons together and firmly burned the memory into her brain that her boss was a threat that made her disconcerting. The horror was indelible in her memory.

Once you find the event that first activated your amygdala, try to alter your perception of the anxiety-triggering situation to help your amygdala unlearn the old unpleasant memory and register a new pleasant memory. To do that, you must face the anxiety trigger again and hope that it does not lead to a vile experience. Doing so repeatedly makes your amygdala learn that the trigger is not a threat and does not require anxiety response. Understandably, people prefer to avoid the situation that makes them anxious. But by avoiding the trigger, your amygdala will never have a chance to alter its memory.

When you expose yourself to facing the anxiety-provoking situation, you absolutely will start with intense anxiety before it slowly subsides. No matter how anxious and uncomfortable you feel, hang in there until your anxiety diminishes. If you choose to escape from the experience, you fail to let your amygdala update its memory. Being anxious is part of the process and necessary for your amygdala to learn the new knowledge you want it to pick up. The more your emotions are aroused, the faster your amygdala learns. Remember, neurons that fire apart wire apart. As you repeatedly expose yourself to the anxiety trigger and you do not receive any unpleasant treatment, your amygdala updates its memory that the previously feared threat is not a threat.

Re-exposing yourself to an anxious experience requires careful planning because you cannot guarantee that you will face a pleasant experience when you try it, and at worst, your experience may be worse than your previous one. When you force yourself to speak again in front of an audience, your amygdala will gradually unlearn its previous association if you do not get belittled. But if you get one, your amygdala strengthens its association, and your anxiety gets worse.

3. Slow breathing

When your amygdala sounds the alarm, there is no stopping it. You can only slow your anxiety response duration by breathing slowly or being mindful. Slow breathing intercepts the amygdala's reaction by decreasing its activation duration.[3] It also decreases the inhibition of your prefrontal cortex, which allows you to start thinking clearly again.

You can't use logic to calm your amygdala down. Slow breathing does a better job to calm it down than anything else. After all, your body knows that you can't be breathing slowly at the presence of a predator. Incorporate slow breathing into your recovery plan to reduce duration of anxiety while you work on the previous two techniques: ***stop ruminating*** and ***update the amygdala's memory.***

STOPPING ***rumination*** helps you reduce the anxiety generated by the prefrontal cortex system; ***updating your amygdala's memory*** helps you stop the anxiety generated by the amygdala system; ***slow breathing*** supports your process to stop ruminating and update your amygdala's memory.

Tackle these together and not one after another. Tackling just one of these will not help you much because the other opposing forces are still present to reshape your brain. You will likely end up back to where you began. Compare your brain to Play-Doh mold. Assume that it is in a round shape now and you want to reshape it to a star shape. If you try only one technique while ignoring the others, you will reshape it to a star shape once and to a round shape more times. At the end, your mold will still resemble more of a round shape.

It is crucial to reduce the amount of anxiety you encounter every day to minimize your overall stress level. We have learned that stress reduces our neurogenesis capacity.

It is not easy to get your amygdala to unlearn undesired associations and your prefrontal cortex to stop ruminating, but working toward fixing these problems is one way to cure your anxiety forever, instead of relying on drugs. Take your time to fix this, and your anxiety will gradually diminish.

We have completed the crucial components of brain plasticity. The next chapter unveils how to plan your life activities to harness the natural fluctuation of brain plasticity for the best shape of your brain.

5

PLAN TO MAXIMIZE BRAIN GROWTH

> When you're finished changing, you're finished.
>
> — Benjamin Franklin

Using what we have learned so far, let's go through the full plan to optimizing your brain's growth through all stages of life.

Pregnancy

The nutrition and lifestyle of the mother affects the fetus's neurogenesis rate.[1]

1. Stay away from processed food during pregnancy. Research showed that eating food with high trans-fat

reduces neurogenesis and BDNF levels in newborns.[2]

2. Minimize the consumption of seafood with a high concentration of mercury. Mercury can damage the developing brain in the fetus.[3]
3. Maintain a good emotional state during pregnancy to allow ideal brain growth for the child. A study found that mothers who showed anxiety and depression symptoms gave birth to infants with less white matter in their brains.[4]
4. Around eighteen weeks of pregnancy, the baby has developed ears and can start listening. If it is possible, avoid as much noise pollution as possible. Take a walk in the park to expose the baby to nature sounds and enhance the baby's neurogenesis. Alternatively, schedule some time to stay in silence and serenity to get an increased boost for the unborn baby's neurogenesis, as well as your own.

Infant (0-2 Years Old)

This is the critical period of neuroplasticity. An infant's brain is like an empty sponge, ready to absorb as much external stimuli as possible. Their brains grow the most during their first two years. If you are not careful, the experiences you feed them can cause long-term problems. They learn a lot more than you realize, even though they don't speak. During this critical period, anything that brings about a traumatic experience to an infant can cause long-term plastic change to the brain.

1. Avoid using physical aggression, like beating or spanking, as the way to handle them. Their brain will learn to use aggression to solve problems or to seek partners who are aggressive.
2. Manage your stress well. Stressful mothers impair their children's prefrontal cortex development.[5]
3. Intuitively, you will want to try your best to protect their heads from any fall to avoid killing some of their neurons.
4. Infants sleep a lot, and they spent more hours in REM stage, which enhances plasticity. Do not deprive them of sleep to maximize their brain growth.
5. It is possible for them to learn many languages. If you speak and teach them multiple languages, they can pick them up faster compared to when they are older. Only the frequently used language(s) will stick as they grow up. Use this critical period of high plasticity to expose them to different languages.
6. Hug, kiss, and cuddle your children often to increase their neurogenesis rate. Shower them with love to support their emotional development.
7. Provide them with supportive and enriched environment. Play, play, and more play.

From Toddler to Puberty (3-20 Years Old)

Children likely will continue to be exposed to a lot of learning during this period, especially as they enter school life. Because of the nature of competitive plasticity, it is often easier to train the children when they are young, before it becomes more difficult for them to unlearn bad habits or to pick up good habits when they are older.

1. As the child grows older, instill a growth mindset in them and show them that they are born with a lot of potential and not fixed with what they are given.
2. Nurture their inquisitive mind, pique their curiosity, and encourage them to learn as much as they can.
3. Continue to touch them by hugging, kissing, and cuddling to increase their neurogenesis rate. Be wary of introducing smartphones to them as those can increase the physical distance between parents and children. Keeping a pet at home is one good way to increase touch exposure for your children.
4. Introduce them to exercising to support neuron growth.
5. As they grow into older children, help them practice the habit of fasting. Not extreme fasting, but a controlled, time-restricted fasting for a brief duration (twelve hours). This might just mean no snacking on any food past the last meal of the day. This will help them grow more neuron cells to facilitate their learning journey.
6. Help them stay away from pornography and limit their screen time and social media exposure, which can rewire their brain negatively.
7. Help your children stay away from junk food so they won't acquire a taste for it. If they have never tasted overly processed food, they will not develop any

addiction around that food. Making them aware early on of the effect of bad food to their brain and health goes a long way toward ensuring they avoid the food even as they grow up.

8. Give them early education on alcohol and caffeine and how they contribute to neurogenesis problems. There is no reason one must drink a cup of coffee to get through the morning if one sleeps enough.

Falling in Love

When you notice that your young adult children are falling in love, stay close with them to go on the emotional roller-coaster with them. If you are close with your children, they should have no problem telling you their feelings. Help them develop a healthy relationship with their partner, and if it turns sour, support them to prevent their mind from going into an undesirable state.

Their brain's plasticity speeds up at this stage, so it is best to continue using it in a good way:

1. Encourage them to continue learning new things and foster good habits, such as exercising and eating well.
2. During this period, it is easy to unlearn any negative associations they may have picked up previously.

Working Adult

I'm assuming you are about working adult age or beyond, so I'll switch the address to you.

It is crucial that you continue to learn even past school life. When you enter the workforce, you would initially be exposed to a lot of new learning. But after some time, as you become more familiarized with your work, things become easier for you, and you no longer need much learning to cope with your job. At this stage, you have stopped learning.

Make a deliberate effort to learn new things, such as new skills that could benefit your work, or a new hobby, or a new language. Read books to expand your knowledge. Your brain starts to prune off unused knowledge. When you stop learning, the pruning speeds up.

Most people start to develop anxiety before they reach middle age. Some develop it earlier, in their late teens. If you notice that you often feel anxious, investigate the source of the anxiety and tackle it fast. Don't let it spiral out of control. When your brain has reshaped into a worrisome brain, it becomes increasingly difficult to address the issue. The earlier you cure it, the earlier you get to enjoy your life.

Retired Adult

After stepping down from a working life, you are apt to go into a more stagnant life. Many people expect their retirement activities as relaxing all day long and binge watching. The notion that you should become lazier when you retire is ill-conceived because doing so leads to a speedy declination of your brain function. With more free time available, pick up new stimulating activities that you enjoy to avoid the erosion of neurons, such as traveling, exploring new hobbies, learning to play a musical instrument, teaching your grandchildren an activity, or writing a book.

If you have been learning throughout your youth, I bet you won't want to stop learning. Letting your brain decay by stopping learning is too much of a sacrifice.

CONCLUSION

You don't need to have class-A genes to master a complex skill. Everyone has the ability to learn anything, no matter how low their IQ is. IQ should not be used as the barrier to dictate whether you can learn something. The plasticity of the brain allows you to improve your brain as time goes by. Embrace the joy of learning. Mold your brain into the best version of yourself, even if you never thought that was possible. It is the best asset you have. Do not accept that aging must be accompanied by an impaired memory function. Enhance your brain now to still enjoy a plethora of activities in old age and save yourself from neurodegenerative diseases.

Life isn't just about doing mental tests or learning something for the sake of stacking up your neurons. It is important that you choose the mental activities that you enjoy and learn things that you really like or are curious about to be happy. If you have any skill that you are striving to master, you seriously can. It may be difficult, but it is possible. There is no denying it.

Be a better version of yourself every day than you were the day before, and compound your knowledge as you grow older. Enjoy the bountiful knowledge that you can learn in life and achieve your peak brain function to bring out the best in you. In your seventies, you can be as productive as you were when you were younger. Be the one to be looked upon for your accumulated lifetime wisdom, instead of treated with disdain.

I hope this book will help you embrace the beauty of learning and make better choices in your daily routine.

Before you go, do you still remember the fourth item of Maslow's hierarchy of needs?

Thank you for reading this book.

KEEP IN TOUCH

If this book benefits you, would you please take a moment to write a review? I would love to read your comments. It makes my day knowing that this book can help you increase your brain power.

Keep in touch with me at said@saidhasyim.com.

If you wish to be notified of my next book update or special promotion, sign up to my mailing list at https://www.saidhasyim.com.

For a limited time and while stocks last, access the bonus material at https://www.saidhasyim.com/peak-brain-plasticity-exclusive if you purchased this book.

ALSO BY SAID HASYIM

Peak Productivity Series

Peak Human Clock: How to Get up Early, Fix Eating Time Schedule, and Improve Exercise Routines to be Highly Productive

Peak Self-Control: Building Strong Willpower to Accomplish Important Goals

Peak Brain Plasticity: Remember What You Want to Remember and Forget What you Can't Forget

Peak Mindset: Apply Realistic Thinking When Studies on Happiness Fail to Make Us Happy

Peak Life's Work: Find Your Gift and Give It Away

ABOUT THE AUTHOR

Said Hasyim is a certified IT project manager with an obsession for finding the best ways to maximize his productivity. After more than a decade of arduous self-experimentation and research into bio-hacks, Said discovered various methods to improve his productivity. Now, he hopes to share his findings with his readers in his *Peak Productivity* book series to unleash their inner potential.

Find out more about Said at www.saidhasyim.com.

facebook.com/SaidHasyimReal
instagram.com/SaidHasyimReal
linkedin.com/in/saidhasyim

NOTES

Introduction

1. *Dementia*. (2020, September 21). WHO. https://www.who.int/newsroom/fact-sheets/detail/dementia

1. Neuroplasticity

1. McLaughlin, K. A., Greif Green, J., Gruber, M. J., Sampson, N. A., Zaslavsky, A. M., & Kessler, R. C. (2012). Childhood adversities and first onset of psychiatric disorders in a national sample of US adolescents. *Archives of General Psychiatry*, *69*(11), 1151. https://doi.org/10.1001/archgenpsychiatry.2011.2277
2. Earp, B. D., Wudarczyk, O. A., Foddy, B., & Savulescu, J. (2017). Addicted to love: What is love addiction and when should it be treated? *Philosophy, psychiatry, & psychology : PPP*, *24*(1), 77–92. https://doi.org/10.1353/ppp.2017.0011
3. Leuner, B., Glasper, E. R., & Gould, E. (2010). Parenting and plasticity. *Trends in Neurosciences*, *33*(10), 465–473. https://doi.org/10.1016/j.tins.2010.07.003
4. Tamana, S. K. et al. (2019). Screen-time is associated with inattention problems in preschoolers: Results from the CHILD birth cohort study. *PLOS ONE*, *14*(4), e0213995. https://doi.org/10.1371/journal.pone.0213995
5. Fancourt, D., & Steptoe, A. (2019). Television viewing and cognitive decline in older age: Findings from the English Longitudinal Study of Aging. *Scientific Reports*, *9*(1), 1. https://doi.org/10.1038/s41598-019-39354-4
6. Statista. (2020, November 24). *Worldwide digital population as of October 2020*. https://www.statista.com/statistics/617136/digital-population-worldwide/
7. Sparrow, B., Liu, J., & Wegner, D. M. (2011). Google effects on memory: Cognitive consequences of having information at our fingertips. *Science*, *333*(6043), 776–778. https://doi.org/10.1126/science.1207745
8. Frishberg, H. (2020, July 17). *Men who watch too much porn more likely to have erectile dysfunction: study*. *New York Post*. https://nypost.-

com/2020/07/17/men-who-watch-porn-more-likely-to-have-erectile-dysfunction-study/

9. Statista. (2020, November 24). *Number of global social network users 2017-2025.* https://www.statista.com/statistics/278414/number-of-worldwide-social-network-users/
10. *Game theory: The effects of video games on the brain.* (2014, July). Brain&Life. https://www.brainandlife.org/articles/how-do-video-games-affect-the-developing-brains-of-children/

2. Neurogenesis

1. Karimian, M., Famitafreshi, H., Fanaei, H., Attari, F., & Fatima, S. (2015). Social isolation is associated with reduced neurogenesis, impaired spatial working memory performance, and altered anxiety levels in male rats. *Open Access Animal Physiology*, 87. https://doi.org/10.2147/oaap.s84327
2. Luo, Y., Hawkley, L. C., Waite, L. J., & Cacioppo, J. T. (2012). Loneliness, health, and mortality in old age: A national longitudinal study. *Social Science & Medicine*, *74*(6), 907–914. https://doi.org/10.1016/j.socscimed.2011.11.028
3. Lu, L. (2003). Modification of hippocampal neurogenesis and neuroplasticity by social environments. *Experimental Neurology*, *183*(2), 600–609. https://doi.org/10.1016/s0014-4886(03)00248-6
4. Bremner J. D. (2006). Stress and brain atrophy. *CNS & neurological disorders drug targets*, *5*(5), 503–512. https://doi.org/10.2174/187152706778559309
5. Han, M. E. et al. (2007). Inhibitory effects of caffeine on hippocampal neurogenesis and function. *Biochemical and Biophysical Research Communications*, *356*(4), 976–980. https://doi.org/10.1016/j.bbrc.2007.03.086
6. Anderson, M. L., Nokia, M. S., Govindaraju, K. P., & Shors, T. J. (2012). Moderate drinking? Alcohol consumption significantly decreases neurogenesis in the adult hippocampus. *Neuroscience*, **224**, 202–209. https://doi.org/10.1016/j.neuroscience.2012.08.018
7. Kohman, R. A., & Rhodes, J. S. (2013). Neurogenesis, inflammation, and behavior. *Brain, Behavior, and Immunity*, *27*, 22–32. https://doi.org/10.1016/j.bbi.2012.09.003
8. Molteni, R., Barnard, R. J., Ying, Z., Roberts, C. K., & Gómez-Pinilla, F. (2002). A high-fat, refined sugar diet reduces hippocampal brain-derived neurotrophic factor, neuronal plasticity, and learning. *Neuroscience*, *112*(4), 803–814. https://doi.org/10.1016/s0306-4522(02)00123-9

9. Sifferlin, A. (2015, September 16). *34 percent of kids eat fast food on a given day, study says*. Time. https://time.com/4035490/fast-food-kids/
10. Chang, L. W. (1977). Neurotoxic effects of mercury—A review. *Environmental Research*, *14*(3), 329–373. https://doi.org/10.1016/0013-9351(77)90044-5
11. Stansfeld, S. A. et al. (2005). Aircraft and road traffic noise and children's cognition and health: a cross-national study. *The Lancet*, *365*(9475), 1942–1949. https://doi.org/10.1016/s0140-6736(05)66660-3
12. Kraus, K. S. et al. (2010). Noise trauma impairs neurogenesis in the rat hippocampus. *Neuroscience*, *167*(4), 1216–1226. https://doi.org/10.1016/j.neuroscience.2010.02.071.
13. Mackes, N. K. et al. (2020). Early childhood deprivation is associated with alterations in adult brain structure despite subsequent environmental enrichment. *Proceedings of the National Academy of Sciences*, *117*(1), 641–649. https://doi.org/10.1073/pnas.1911264116
14. Cox, S. R. et al. (2016). Associations between education and brain structure at age 73, adjusted for age 11 IQ. *Neurology*, *87*(17), 1820–1826. https://doi.org/10.1212/WNL.0000000000003247
15. Sharp, E. S., & Gatz, M. (2011). Relationship between education and dementia. *Alzheimer Disease & Associated Disorders*, *25*(4), 289–304. https://doi.org/10.1097/wad.0b013e318211c83c
16. Stein, M., Winkler, C., Kaiser, A., & Dierks, T. (2014). Structural brain changes related to bilingualism: Does immersion make a difference? *Frontiers in Psychology*, *5*, 1. https://doi.org/10.3389/fpsyg.2014.01116
17. Baik, S. H., Rajeev, V., Fann, D. Y., Jo, D. G., & Arumugam, T. V. (2020). Intermittent fasting increases adult hippocampal neurogenesis. *Brain and behavior*, *10*(1), e01444. https://doi.org/10.1002/brb3.1444
18. Goekint, M. et al. (2010). Strength training does not influence serum brain-derived neurotrophic factor. *European Journal of Applied Physiology*, *110*(2), 285–293. https://doi.org/10.1007/s00421-010-1461-3
19. Marston, K. J. et al. (2017). Intense resistance exercise increases peripheral brain-derived neurotrophic factor. *Journal of Science and Medicine in Sport*, *20*(10), 899–903. https://doi.org/10.1016/j.jsams.2017.03.015
20. Huang, Y. Q. et al. (2018). Effects of voluntary wheel-running types on hippocampal neurogenesis and spatial cognition in middle-aged mice. *Frontiers in cellular neuroscience*, *12*, 177. https://doi.org/10.3389/fncel.2018.00177
21. Florida State University. (2017, April 17). Think brain games make you smarter? Think again, researchers say: New study finds no evidence

games increase overall cognitive abilities. *ScienceDaily*. Retrieved January 10, 2021 from www.sciencedaily.com/releases/2017/04/170417095528.htm

22. Wan, C. Y., & Schlaug, G. (2010). Music-making as a tool for promoting brain plasticity across the life span. *The Neuroscientist: a review journal bringing neurobiology, neurology and psychiatry*, 16(5), 566–577. https://doi.org/10.1177/1073858410377805
23. Shah, C., Erhard, K., Ortheil, H. J., Kaza, E., Kessler, C., & Lotze, M. (2013). Neural correlates of creative writing: An fMRI study. *Human brain mapping*, *34*(5), 1088–1101. https://doi.org/10.1002/hbm.21493
24. Kirste, I., Nicola, Z., Kronenberg, G., Walker, T. L., Liu, R. C., & Kempermann, G. (2013). Is silence golden? Effects of auditory stimuli and their absence on adult hippocampal neurogenesis. *Brain Structure and Function*, *220*(2), 1221–1228. https://doi.org/10.1007/s00429-013-0679-3
25. Mueller, A. D., Meerlo, P., McGinty, D., & Mistlberger, R. E. (2015). Sleep and adult neurogenesis: Implications for cognition and mood. *Current topics in behavioral neurosciences*, *25*, 151–181. https://doi.org/10.1007/7854_2013_251
26. Meerlo, P., Mistlberger, R. E., Jacobs, B. L., Heller, H. C., & McGinty, D. (2009). New neurons in the adult brain: The role of sleep and consequences of sleep loss. *Sleep medicine reviews*, *13*(3), 187–194. https://doi.org/10.1016/j.smrv.2008.07.004/
27. Shechter, R., Baruch, K., Schwartz, M., & Rolls, A. (2011). Touch gives new life: Mechanosensation modulates spinal cord adult neurogenesis. *Molecular psychiatry*, 16(3), 342–352. https://doi.org/10.1038/mp.2010.116
28. University of Calgary. (2013, May 1). New brain research shows two parents may be better than one. *ScienceDaily*. Retrieved January 9, 2021 from www.sciencedaily.com/releases/2013/05/130501193202.htm
29. Yamamoto, T., Hirayama, A., Hosoe, N., Furube, M., & Hirano, S. (2009). Soft-Diet feeding inhibits adult neurogenesis in hippocampus of mice. *The Bulletin of Tokyo Dental College*, *50*(3), 117–124. https://doi.org/10.2209/tdcpublication.50.117
30. Mitome, M., Hasegawa, T., & Shirakawa, T. (2005). Mastication influences the survival of newly generated cells in mouse dentate gyrus. *Neuroreport*, *16*(3), 249–252. https://doi.org/10.1097/00001756-200502280-00009
31. Blennow, K., Hardy, J., & Zetterberg, H. (2012). The neuropathology and neurobiology of traumatic brain injury. *Neuron*, *76*(5), 886–899. https://doi.org/10.1016/j.neuron.2012.11.021
32. Mez, J., Daneshvar et al. (2017). Clinicopathological evaluation of chronic traumatic encephalopathy in players of American football. *JAMA*, *318*(4), 360. https://doi.org/10.1001/jama.2017.8334

33. Morissette, M. P., Prior, H. J., Tate, R. B., Wade, J., & Leiter, J. R. S. (2020). Associations between concussion and risk of diagnosis of psychological and neurological disorders: A retrospective population-based cohort study. *Family Medicine and Community Health*, *8*(3), 1. https://doi.org/10.1136/fmch-2020-000390
34. Herrera, D. G. et al. (2003). Selective impairment of hippocampal neurogenesis by chronic alcoholism: Protective effects of an antioxidant. *Proceedings of the National Academy of Sciences of the United States of America*, *100*(13), 7919–7924. https://doi.org/10.1073/pnas.1230907100

3. Maximize Learning

1. https://oxford.universitypressscholarship.com/view/10.1093/acprof:oso/9780198574002.001.0001/acprof-9780198574002
2. https://www.sciencedirect.com/science/article/pii/B9780128009000000087
3. Zhang, H., Miller, K., Cleveland, R., & Cortina, K. (2018). How listening to music affects reading: Evidence from eye tracking. *Journal of experimental psychology. Learning, memory, and cognition*, *44*(11), 1778–1791. https://doi.org/10.1037/xlm0000544
4. *Calculators in the classroom.* https://sedl.org/pubs/quick-takes/qt_calculators.pdf
5. Murre, J. M., & Dros, J. (2015). Replication and analysis of Ebbinghaus' forgetting curve. *PloS one*, *10*(7), e0120644. https://doi.org/10.1371/journal.pone.0120644
6. Mcleod, S. (2014). *Loftus and Palmer.* SimplyPsychology. https://www.simplypsychology.org/loftus-palmer.html

4. Rewire an Anxious Brain

1. *Investing in treatment for depression and anxiety leads to fourfold return.* (2016, April 13). WHO. https://www.who.int/news/item/13-04-2016-investing-in-treatment-for-depression-and-anxiety-leads-to-fourfold-return
2. University of Colorado at Boulder. (2018, December 10). Your brain on imagination: It's a lot like reality, study shows. *ScienceDaily*. Retrieved January 10, 2021 from www.sciencedaily.com/releases/2018/12/181210144943.htm

3. Ma, X. et al. (2017). The effect of diaphragmatic breathing on attention, negative affect, and stress in healthy adults. *Frontiers in psychology*, *8*, 874. https://doi.org/10.3389/fpsyg.2017.00874

5. Plan to Maximize Brain Growth

1. Cheatham, C. L. (2019). Nutritional factors in fetal and infant brain development. *Annals of Nutrition and Metabolism*, *75*(1), 20–32. https://doi.org/10.1159/000508052
2. Sullivan, E. L., Nousen, E. K., Chamlou, K. A., & Grove, K. L. (2012). The impact of maternal high-fat diet consumption on neural development and behavior of offspring. *International Journal of Obesity Supplements*, 2(S2), S7–S13. https://doi.org/10.1038/ijosup.2012.15
3. *Methylmercury and Human Embryonic Development*. (2016, April 18). The Embryo Project Encyclopedia. https://embryo.asu.edu/pages/methylmercury-and-human-embryonic-development
4. Dean, D. C. et al. (2018). Association of prenatal maternal depression and anxiety symptoms with infant white matter microstructure. *JAMA Pediatrics*, *172*(10), 973. https://doi.org/10.1001/jamapediatrics.2018.2132
5. Nadel, J., Soussignan, R., Canet, P., Libert, G., & Gérardin, P. (2005). Two-month-old infants of depressed mothers show mild, delayed, and persistent change in emotional states after non-contingent interaction. *Infant Behavior and Development*, *28*(4), 418–425. https://doi.org/10.1016/j.infbeh.2005.03.005

www.ingramcontent.com/pod-product-compliance
Ingram Content Group UK Ltd.
Pitfield, Milton Keynes, MK11 3LW, UK
UKHW021657190726
13853UKWH00001B/327